Abusive People

Recognize Manipulative and Emotionally Abusive People

(Discover How to Identify and Protect Yourself From All Forms of Abusive)

Gregory Moffett

Published By **Tyson Maxwell**

Gregory Moffett

All Rights Reserved

Abusive People: Recognize Manipulative and Emotionally Abusive People (Discover How to Identify and Protect Yourself From All Forms of Abusive)

ISBN 978-1-7388580-0-2

No part of this guidebook shall be reproduced in any form without permission in writing from the publisher except in the case of brief quotations embodied in critical articles or reviews.

Legal & Disclaimer

The information contained in this book is not designed to replace or take the place of any form of medicine or professional medical advice. The information in this book has been provided for educational & entertainment purposes only.

The information contained in this book has been compiled from sources deemed reliable, and it is accurate to the best of the Author's knowledge; however, the Author cannot guarantee its accuracy and validity and cannot be held liable for any errors or omissions. Changes are periodically made to this book. You must consult your doctor or get professional medical advice before using any of the suggested remedies, techniques, or information in this book.

Upon using the information contained in this book, you agree to hold harmless the Author from and against any damages, costs, and expenses, including any legal fees potentially resulting from the application of any of the information provided by this guide. This disclaimer applies to any damages or injury caused by the use and application, whether directly or indirectly, of any advice or information presented, whether for breach of contract, tort, negligence, personal injury, criminal intent, or under any other cause of action.

You agree to accept all risks of using the information presented inside this book. You need to consult a professional medical practitioner in order to ensure you are both able and healthy enough to participate in this program.

Table Of Contents

Chapter 1: What Is Narcissistic Personality Disorder (Npd)? 1

Chapter 2: How To Spot An Overt Narcissist.................. 9

Chapter 3: What Is A Covert Narcissist? . 19

Chapter 4: What Is Communal Narcissism? 29

Chapter 5: What Is A Malignant Narcissist? Signs, Causes, & How To Deal With One 48

Chapter 6: Eight Steps To Overcoming Your Narcissism.............. 65

Chapter 7: How To Be Less Controlling .. 87

Chapter 8: Real Life Truth About Selfishness 96

Chapter 9: Dealing With Selfishness..... 103

Chapter 10: The Selfish Me Uncovered 105

Chapter 11: Looking Closer On The Selfish Me 119

Chapter 12: Understanding Selfishness 122

Chapter 13: Characteristics Of Selfishness 126

Chapter 14: Understanding Selfish People 131

Chapter 15: Why Stop Being Selfish 134

Chapter 16: How To Stop Being Selfish 136

Chapter 17: Terminating The Toxicity In Your Life.. 146

Chapter 18: Toxic Traits 153

Chapter 19: Toxic Taxonomy (The Noxious Nine).. 165

Chapter 20: The Toxic Wheel Of Misfortune 169

Chapter 1: What Is Narcissistic Personality Disorder (Npd)?

Narcissistic Personality Disorder

Self-significance, lack of empathy, and a continual pattern of inner enjoy and conduct are all inclinations of narcissistic character sickness (NPD).

Many highbrow health specialists use the Diagnostic and Statistical Manual of Mental Illnesses (DSM-five) to diagnose this and one-of-a-kind troubles. It is one in each of numerous top notch forms of personality troubles which might be diagnosed with the useful useful resource of this guide.

In phrases of functioning, the infection significantly impairs the character and is located through some of different hard persona abilities. Similar to distinctive person troubles, this one has a destructive have an effect on on social, familial, and expert connections similarly to different factors of lifestyles.

Symptoms of Narcissistic Personality Disorder

An inflated feel of self, a craving for hobby all the time, being self-targeted, missing empathy, and being preoccupied with energy and achievement are five trends of narcissism. Among the NPD signs and signs are some of the subsequent:

Constant preference for attention, validation, and praise

Belief that one is first-rate or precise and should best interact with human beings of the identical popularity

Overconfidence in a single's abilities and accomplishments

Using some other character for one's very personal advantage

Having an envied feeling or wondering that others have envied them

Lacking of compassion for others

Persistent delusions of undertaking strength and achievement

Obsession with function or achievement

Feelings of entitlement and the choice for preferential remedy

You can be able to understand whether or now not a person has NPD with the aid of manner of looking for a number of those signs and symptoms. People with narcissistic personality disease are commonly described as arrogant, immodest, self-targeted, and haughty. Because they trust themselves as advanced to others, they regularly insist on proudly owning objects that mirror a successful lifestyle.

Despite this exaggerated self-photo, they are reliant on constant praise and interest to boost their vanity. As a surrender cease end result, people with narcissistic man or woman illness are generally very sensitive to criticism, it truly is frequently appeared as a private assault.

Narcissism vs. NPD

The term "narcissism" is often used to symbolize individuals who appear to care greater about themselves than about one of a kind people. Four However, now not absolutely all people with those traits has a man or woman sickness. While narcissistic developments also can once in a while be popular, inclusive of within the course of youth, this does not guarantee that someone will later accumulate NPD.

Narcissistic personality sickness analysis

Only a skilled intellectual fitness professional is certified to make an legitimate analysis, and this character have to show off impairments in person functioning across some of domain names, which include a grandiose experience of self-significance and interpersonal demanding situations with hobby-seeking out, empathy, and intimacy.

To gain a deeper information of someone's signs and signs and symptoms, several questionnaires and character exams may be performed. The International Personality Disorder Examination (IPDE) and the Narcissistic Personality Inventory are two exams regularly used to grow to be privy to narcissistic character illness (NPI).

Additionally, man or woman feature and trait impairments have to be sturdy through the years and in various contexts; they must now not be everyday for the man or woman's lifestyle, surroundings, or developmental diploma; and they must now not be right now associated with substance use or a present day day scientific state of affairs.

How To Identify A Malignant Narcissist

Prevalence of NPD

According to the National Institute of Mental Health, nine.1% of American adults come across at least one shape of persona illness every twelve months. Older estimates placed the prevalence of narcissistic personality sickness mainly at 6.2% of American adults,6 but more modern-day facts endorse that the superiority fees may be lower than within the starting idea.

According to estimates, 0.Five% to 5% of people inside the United States suffer from narcissistic individual illness.

7 Men are much more likely than ladies to revel in NPD.

In contrast to exclusive man or woman issues together with borderline person ailment, delinquent man or woman disease, and histrionic character disorder, narcissistic man or woman infection is regarded to be a outstanding deal less regular.

Causes of Narcissistic Personality Disorder

While the right etiology of the contamination is unknown, experts have located some capability contributing variables. Narcissistic individual infection is considered to be inspired with the useful resource of some of adolescence events, along with:

Trauma or abuse

Excessive acclaim

Absence of a actual validation surroundings

Parents who consume an excessive amount of

Erratic parenting

Despite the truth that the right motives are in all likelihood diverse and variable, genetics and biology also are assumed to have a enormous effect.

Types of Narcissistic Personality Disorder

While the DSM-5 would not separate among severa types of the circumstance, there is evidence that the outflow of aspect outcomes can change notably. A few professionals have proposed that there are some difficulty like discernable subtypes of NPD:

Pretentious, easy selfishness is described via intensity, presumption, and affected man or woman attributes. Individuals with this form of NPD are certain to need compassion, act forcefully, take gain of others, and take part in hotshot strategies of behaving.

Helpless, undercover selfishness is defined through touchiness and protectiveness. Individuals with this shape of NPD might look for endorsement, but socially pull out on the off threat that it is not given. They can also likewise come across low self assurance.

Other proposed subtypes consist of hypervigilant and advanced self-absorption. Individuals with the hypervigilant type are portrayed as folks that revel in shame, unreasonable responsiveness, and handily damage feelings. Those with the advanced type are depicted as displaying up normally usually with problems focused on the absence of compassion, a penchant for narcissism, and self-centeredness.

Types of Narcissism

There are likewise numerous forms of self-absorption that an character may additionally additionally display. The primary types of self-absorption are overt, covert, unfavorable, communal, and malignant. Showing such a styles of selfishness could no longer guarantee to signify that an individual has the self-absorbed behavioral state of affairs.

Chapter 2: How To Spot An Overt Narcissist

Narcissistic Personality

How to Spot an Overt Narcissist

It also can astound you, however, there are numerous sorts of self-absorption.

There is the covert narcissist who attempts to hide their self-targeted controls.

Covert narcissists frequently slip thru the cracks and their state of affairs is undiscovered.

And in some time, there may be the unmistakable egotist who's shameless and unashamed of their self-centeredness and craving for attention.

But, there are numerous attributes and developments of the overt narcissist that lead them to attractive to different humans.

The overt narcissist, at the same time as poisonous to connections, is regularly equipped to encircle themselves with admirers, companions, and doormats.

In this book, we can have a look at four symptoms and symptoms and signs and symptoms of an overt narcissist, and why those behaviors frequently purpose them to so charismatic and suitable.

How To Spot An Overt Narcissist: Lack Of Empathy

Empathy is absent from overt narcissists.

Sympathy and empathy are not the equal.

Feeling unhappy for someone is sympathy. Empathy is the actual capacity to put oneself in a few unique person's scenario and recognize their warfare or struggling.

The overt narcissist is certainly too self-absorbed and believes they are in a superior characteristic to others to be empathetic.

Other individuals are best a technique to an cease for an overt narcissist for the purpose that they're incapable of feeling empathy.

The overt narcissist frequently has a massive amount of near pals, which also can make a contribution to their charming appearance.

The overt narcissist often gives a very appealing persona, whole of buddies and fans. Others are interested in them due to this.

Problematically, the overt narcissist has few, if any, actual friends.

"Friends" are nothing greater than admirers, sycophants, or groupies to the overt narcissist.

You can't find out real love or friendship in case you lack empathy.

Although the overt narcissist refers to you as a pal, you're absolutely honestly a follower.

How To Spot An Overt Narcissist: Charming

A narcissist is typically portrayed as an A-type bully who is rude and opinionated.

The overt narcissist, but, is frequently endearing, slick-speakme, and likeable.

Keep in mind that the overt narcissist stories horrible arrogance regardless of their grandiose demeanor.

The overt narcissist need persistent validation and high fine confirmation. Others step in at this issue!

It is an act for a blatant narcissist to be fascinating.

A cunning mask is worn by using using an overt narcissist after they show problem or maybe interest in others.

The overt narcissist in no manner well-knownshows proper attraction, generosity, or kindness.

The overt narcissist is preoccupied with their public character, which often includes seeming to be a exquisite humanitarian.

A blatant narcissist is professional at deceiving. They can also gift as suitable listeners, givers, compassionate, loving, and reliable.

These developments account for the popularity of overt narcissists.

While simultaneously bringing human beings into their inner circle and retaining them at a distance, the overt narcissist.

How to Spot an Overt Narcissist: Demands Admiration

The overt narcissist will solicit your reward at the same time as feigning friendship with you.

Being in a dating with an overt narcissist calls for admiration and appreciation.

This suggests that the overt narcissist may not make the effort to con you or persuade you to praise them.

Any type of reference to an overt narcissist need to encompass admiration, validation, and praise.

The overt narcissist will make it easy that they want accolades.

The overt narcissist can even offer you with recommendation on a way to praise them of their want.

The overt narcissist frequently uses verbal and emotional abuse as a tool to set up and keep relationships.

However, due to the fact the overt narcissist often has an oversized individual, people will positioned up with abuse simply to be round them.

How To Spot An Overt Narcissist: Hard Working/Successful

The fact that an overt narcissist is frequently prosperous, a success, and capable of offer blessings of relationships is some different factor at play.

The overt narcissist frequently works tough and achieves achievement.

Being taken into consideration as "a success" thru others performs a role in the overt narcissist's want to seem massive-than-lifestyles.

Many people locate success and cash to be attractive. Because of this, the overt narcissist is immensely appealing as a pal and a romantic partner.

The overt narcissist gives human beings greater than without a doubt their winning attraction; furthermore they get bonuses and further privileges.

The overt narcissist is often content material material to unfold riches. Weekends spent at their lakeside domestic, exceptional eating, steeply-priced cars, toys, and plenty of others.

Hard difficult work produces earnings, wealth produces cloth devices, and people trap others inside the route of the overt narcissist.

But maintain in mind that an overt narcissist's generosity is never free.

The overt narcissist will constantly name for his or her due, your admire, and admiration.

Additionally, in case you reject a blatant narcissist, you would probably undergo top notch repercussions in addition to having to transport with out.

An overt narcissist might frequently make the most their coins and standing to pursue retribution if they're no longer shown appreciate and appreciation.

You may not be capable of quick save you the fan membership of buddies and fans of an overt narcissist.

Because in case you leave a blatant narcissist, others have to do the equal and display the facade.

Be conscious, in case you shatter the general public character of an overt narcissist, they'll try and ostracize you from buddies, family, and distinctive valuable relationships.

How To Spot An Overt Narcissist: Shallow Relationships

A superficial connection is the best shape of relationship an overt narcissist may additionally additionally have.

Keep in thoughts that the overt narcissist is a expert actor.

So wonderful that the overt narcissist may skip for an obedient companion, a long-lasting friend, or a dependable mentor.

To preserve manipulate over their relationships, the overt narcissist must cause them to quick and superficial.

Making oneself on hand, to be had, and open to positive grievance is a name for for real love and friendship. The overt narcissist disregards they all.

Must be in rate should be the overt narcissist. The reason of all narcissism is manipulation.

A blatant narcissist goals the relationship to be brief so that you can give you their approval or permit you to pass if crucial.

The overt narcissist in the end perspectives all connections as disposable.

Conclusion

People regularly appearance as lots as or aspire to be the overt narcissist due to the truth they are the lifestyles of the birthday celebration.

The overt narcissist is frequently seemed as charismatic, endearing, and type but their abusive tendencies.

However, the risks of being in a dating with a blatant narcissist are brilliant.

Many humans are victimized through the ever-charming overt narcissist, who abuses their minds, emotions, or minds' feelings.

Please get expert assist if you or someone is in an abusive courting with a blatant narcissist.

The best person to provide steering and useful resource within the recovery method is a licensed expert counselor.

Chapter 3: What Is A Covert Narcissist?

What Is A Covert Narcissist?

Table of Contents

You must see an overt narcissist as someone who is pompous, attention-searching for, and haughty at the identical time as you keep in mind a narcissist. But covert narcissism is likewise a shape of narcissism, it is less obvious. These narcissists can also additionally furthermore display off much less overt signs and symptoms and signs and symptoms of the sickness, making them more difficult to pick out, however they in spite of the fact that display off an high-quality choice for reward and adoration in addition to a stylish lack of empathy for others.

Read right now to research more approximately covert narcissism and its most common tendencies.

What Is a Covert Narcissist?

Covert narcissism—additionally referred to as willing narcissism—has been defined due to the fact the "greater silent and subtle model" of narcissism. This type of narcissist stocks the identical overarching tendencies of the persona sickness—an inflated sense of self, a loss of empathy for others and an immoderate want for admiration and interest—but manifests the ones tendencies in a much less apparent manner.

Differences Between Covert Narcissists and Overt Narcissists

Overt narcissists regularly display off immoderate self-esteem and extraversion, however covert narcissists often display off low vanity, that might reason defensiveness, insecurities, and self-interest. However, covert narcissists retain to have an exaggerated view of themselves and lack empathy for others.

Furthermore, it's far been determined that overt narcissism is often more associated with extraversion and in addition ranges of agreeableness, however covert narcissism is determined to have a larger association with introversion and neuroticism.

David M. Reiss, a psychiatrist who has been in workout for greater than 30 years and is set up in Rancho Santa Fe, California, believes that there can be variations in the quantity of self-recognition amongst covert and overt narcissists. According to Reiss, women and men with overt narcissism may not be aware of or capable of recognize their conduct, even as people with covert narcissism may be able to sense empathy and feature a experience of proper and incorrect, if pleasant in short.

Causes Of Covert Narcissism

Although some research has decided out that there can be a hereditary tendency toward the scenario, the right beginning location of covert narcissism remains doubtful. Reiss asserts that personality problems like covert narcissism, which is probably frequently not inherited, can cease result from early trauma and someone's sensitivity to that trauma, similarly to from greater extreme disruptive conduct or defenses.

Indeed, it has been proposed that environmental variables like strain or traumatic adolescence sports, at the aspect of destructive encounters or excessive praise, may additionally moreover additionally feature potential triggers for narcissistic character disorder. Personality, temperament, and neurobiology—the link between one's thoughts and movements—are extraordinary viable contributing elements.

Signs Of A Covert Narcissist

In phrases of exaggerated self-significance and a loss of empathy for others, covert narcissists exhibit the same important inclinations as overt narcissists. However, there are precise characteristics of covert narcissism, and the pathology that underlies them manifests in diverse techniques.

Although terrific humans may moreover display off first-rate hidden narcissistic dispositions, the subsequent are everyday signs and symptoms and symptoms and signs and symptoms:

Introversion

Covert narcissism has been decided to correlate pretty with introversion. This diverges from overt narcissism, which commonly entails extra grandiose suggests and extraverted conduct. Rather than appearing in a brash, direct manner, the covert narcissist may additionally moreover display a quieter feel of superiority and seem more reserved.

Self-Consciousness and Social Insecurity

When a person has covert narcissism, they'll will be predisposed to enjoy victimized, which in a manner expresses their feeling of region of expertise and superiority. Because they regularly display off extreme sensitivity and might struggle with terrible conceitedness, covert narcissists may additionally regularly are looking for approval from others. Due to their fragile sense of self, people with covert narcissism additionally have a tendency to be exceptionally touchy to complaint and can be more inclined to absorb it.

Defensiveness and Anger

Covert narcissists are much more likely to show "narcissistic rage"—a unethical inside the course of hostility and anger. Research shows that is because of the reality covert narcissists have a tendency to be quite neurotic, at the equal time as overt narcissists are normally more strong emotionally[1].

Passive Aggressiveness

While covert narcissists are much more likely to stay inside the records, overt narcissists frequently hog the limelight. When interacting, covert narcissists may additionally moreover use extra passive-competitive strategies like guilt trips, accidental compliments, and veiled hostility jokes. They may opt to use those strategies over direct battle selection.

Gaslighting

According to Reiss, a not unusual covert narcissist approach is gaslighting, a form of highbrow manipulation that makes the victim doubt their non-public perceptions, mind, and memories. He says that due to the fact narcissists have the propensity to vicinity blame on others, you could feel as even though some issue isn't always quite proper.

"Check yourself. It's a terrific concept to take a close to have a look at each events in a dating if your reaction to someone is largely being gaslighted—amazed and astonished that this is happening, he provides.

How To Deal With A Covert Narcissist

The first-class safety in opposition to enticing with a narcissist, in keeping with Reiss, is to set up business enterprise, high-quality limits.

Realize that you can now not pass very a long way trying to purpose with a narcissist or someone whose narcissistic tendencies are showing whilst you are attractive with them. Simply set up limits. When someone truly cares approximately themselves, you can not argue with them, steady with Reiss.

It's better to just adhere on your limits and deliver your self a tremendous quantity of place at the same time as someone is in this temper. You might be able to have a talk to address the hassle and communicate up for your self, relying on whether or no longer or now not the alternative character admits that their conduct is beside the issue.

When To Ask For Help

It can be a first rate concept to get professional assist in case you're having problem coping with a covert narcissist or if you count on you'll likely have covert narcissism your self. You also can examine greater approximately what to expect from the contamination and the way to set obstacles in relationships with the aid of using running with a mental fitness expert. The proper information is that there can be typically want for healing because of the truth narcissistic character problems are curable ailments. Focusing on what you can control is the important element.

The behavior of the alternative person is "hitting your susceptible locations" if it reasons worry, melancholy, unjustified guilt, or a lack of vanity, constant with Reiss. Although you can't lead them to act higher, on the lookout for expert assist facilitates lessen your susceptibility to feeling terrible once they do.

Antagonistic Narcissism: The Dark Side of Overt Narcissism

This is the element of narcissism we hate the maximum.

Known as a spectrum disorder, narcissism. The behaviors tested via narcissists range from obnoxious however healthy to pathologically risky. There are number one types of narcissism: overt and covert, as turned into included in in advance sections. Overt narcissism is characterised thru grandiose conduct, excessive self-love, and a want for adulation. Insecurity, timidity, and a loss of self-warranty are dispositions of covert narcissism. Today, we're going to talk approximately detrimental narcissism, a less commonplace subtype of overt narcissism.

Aggressive and manipulative conduct are traits of hostile narcissists. They often manage others to reap their goals and haven't any qualms about taking advantage of others. They are also very aggressive and usually demand the spotlight. Narcissists who're against others can reason a number of harm to every themselves and those round them.

Abuse, every emotionally and bodily, is common among people with opposed narcissism. They make use of their role and strength to make existence ugly for others spherical them, and they find out large satisfaction in their patients' struggling.

Some common behaviors associated with antagonistic narcissism encompass:

Constant criticism and belittling of others

Excessive needs for hobby and compliance

Threats or real physical violence

Manipulation and exploitation for personal advantage.

If you are in a courting with someone who famous those behaviors, it may be very tough to interrupt out. It is vital to consider that you are not accountable for someone else's behavior, and also you need to be handled with recognize. Seek assist from friends, circle of relatives, or a professional if you cannot leave the scenario in your private. Remember, you aren't by myself.

Chapter 4: What Is Communal Narcissism?

Although it isn't diagnosed as a proper evaluation, communal narcissism refers to grandiose, inflated perceptions interior a communal surroundings.1 Communal narcissists regularly consider they have first-rate social abilties and excessive tiers of likeability and helpfulness. In truth, they are pretty hypocritical, as most in their recognition facilities on assembly their very personal intrinsic goals.

What Is Communal Narcissism?

The complicated infection of narcissistic character sickness is a continuum, and severa capabilities display up in awesome strategies counting on the character and situation. Particularly folks who be with the aid of communal narcissism will be inclined to overstate their ability for and mastery of social abilties. They anticipate they have got great potential and functionality, often questioning they may be the area's high-quality mother and father, listeners, or charitable people.

Pax Robertson, Ph.D., Professor for the Department of Psychology of Washington State UniversityChris Barry, Ph.D., Professor for the Department of Psychology of Washington State University explains, "Someone with communal narcissism will become stuck up within the idea of being specific or remarkable in service to others. Communalism (minus the narcissism) is probably a suitable element (e.G., being excellent, being worried about social problems, being sincere, worrying for others). However, communal narcissism has that added detail of truly grandiose presentations of 1's communalism and promoting oneself as being more communal than others. Examples can be, 'I am the fine buddy someone must have,' 'I am the most useful individual I apprehend,' and 'I might be capable of resolve global poverty.'"[7]

Do Communal Narcissists Actually Care About Their Community?

We all display off some degree of psychological egoism, according to many philosophers and scientists, because of this that all of us act in strategies which might be delivered about thru our non-public self-pursuits. 2 However, folks that be afflicted via narcissistic personality infection have extra feelings of entitlement and superiority. They regularly emerge as consumed with the aid of the use of their very very own success goals. They frequently have trouble empathetically spotting others' real desires and might be hesitant or now not capable of carry out that. Therefore, notwithstanding the reality that they remember they will be doing a incredible gadget of serving their community, this notion can be wrong from the begin.

What Are The Signs of a Communal Narcissist?

Those who be afflicted by way of communal narcissism regularly fee playing giant roles in society. They often experience compelled to "repair" subjects that they don't forget need solving considering that doing so gives them a extremely good revel in of fulfillment. However, their obsessive pursuit of such power may be demanding and dangerous to others.

Communal narcissism can also additionally show up as:

Extreme dedication to specific charities or reasons: Because in their zeal, they may forget about wonderful important jobs or step on human beings's ft.

Often speakme approximately having a assignment or a calling: They keep in mind serving the community to be of severe significance, and they'll deem a few other pastimes as petty or egocentric.

Stirring extra drama or war at charitable or work-related occasions: Rather than attention on carrying out a communal motive, they may be extra focused on hierarchies or self-inflicted politics.

Coming during as a martyr: They will mock or degrade individuals who do not additionally percent the equal martyr-like pursuits (i.E. If they will be a vegan, they will lash out at those who consume meat. Or, they may "hate" rich people who do not donate maximum in their wealth).

Believing they are the excellent at some element: They can also don't have any proof to verify this claim (and others might probably vehemently disagree with it).

Only seeming to expose trouble for societal desires in public: In private, they do now not show off the same motivations. For example, they will donate lavish portions of coins at an crucial occasion, but they wouldn't ever keep in thoughts becoming an nameless donor. Or, they may post approximately desiring to maintain the planet on social media with out truly creating a personal strive to accomplish that.

Examples of Communal Narcissism

Communal narcissism may additionally additionally look precise counting on the state of affairs. Here are some examples of the way it could take region:

At Work

A communal narcissist also can attempt to finish your responsibilities for you at paintings because of the truth they accept as right with they'll be being "beneficial." They also can need to expect they're the handiest difficulty keeping the company collectively and that with out them, the entirety will just disintegrate. Additionally, they frequently look down on coworkers who take day off or act disinterested of their artwork.

Volunteering for a Cause

They ought to try and bypass beyond their authority as volunteers and assume duties even with out the critical education. They have to create controversy at charitable occasions and pay attention excessively on little things in desire to giving priority to the volunteer paintings itself. They regularly take note of how a remarkable deal exceptional humans make investments inside the cause, either in terms of time or cash (and pick out them therefore).

Sports Games

Instead of focusing on honing their personal capabilities, they're aiming to educate others the way to enhance their competencies even as playing a recreation. They appear alternatively inclined to help, ostensibly for the sake of the crew, but they do not take guidance or endorse properly themselves.

Support Groups

In a resource agency like a contemporary mothers enterprise, a communal narcissist may be dispensing unsolicited recommendation to really each person in the organisation, with the concept that they're being "useful."

5 Ways to Deal With a Communal Narcissist

Undoubtedly, coping with narcissism may be traumatic for cherished ones. It's crucial to educate your self on the infection, its signs and signs and symptoms, and to be had remedies. Knowing this can make you experience more on pinnacle of factors of your interactions. Remember which you are never required to position up with any abuse or disrespect as a favored rule.

Here are 5 techniques for managing a set narcissist:

1. Try not to Attempt to Defy Clashing Ways of behaving

While you may in all likelihood revel in enticed to task any man or woman's affection, this circulate pretty regularly misfires. Individuals with selfishness will pretty regularly grow to be defensive and livid even as given input (irrespective of whether or not it's miles valuable).

All subjects taken into consideration, abstaining from expressing some thing the least bit is higher. They would in all likelihood participate in one-of-a-type gaslighting techniques to make up for his or her egotistical fury. For example, they may preserve lying and it is evenhanded to name for their fact. Or but, they could strive to persuade you that you're blended up or in any case create a few troubles.

2. Remain Consistent with Your Qualities

Attempt to try no longer to permit humans to allow you to apprehend the way you need to suppose or revel in. You can assume often approximately your close by place with out feeling pressured to do as such. Somebody with collective selfishness may additionally additionally disparage or shame you for "no longer doing what is crucial" or "feeling sufficiently lively." Recollect that you are your character, and also you reserve every choice to seeking out after the capabilities and necessities which might be influential for you.

three. Limit Setting off Connections

At least, it thoroughly can be beneficial to lessen how hundreds time you spend together, restricting your functionality to expose into their inventory. For instance, assuming which you recognize you may go to activities wherein their conduct will agitate you, positioned down fantastic barriers for your self. Consent to awareness on absolutely a selected willpower or take into account possible unique options.

four. Carry out Limits

You can and need to set limitations on your relationship. In doing as such, keep in mind that you do now not want to acknowledge sick-bred language or analysis from others. Limits shift, however you may remember the accompanying instance scripts:

I am no longer speaking about this depend any in addition.

That isn't a few detail I am inclined to do.

If you query me another time, I will need you to leave my domestic.

This depend isn't always up for discussion.

5. Work on Continuous Taking care of oneself

It's now not hard to become being overpowered, livid, or responsive at the same time as you experience self-targeted behavior. Notwithstanding, it's critical the middle spherical how you can protect your prosperity paying little heed to a few exclusive individual's activities.

Taking care of oneself can encompass collaborating in more care, tracking down tremendous assist, and avowing your self regularly. It likewise includes your physical and close to-to-domestic prosperity by getting sufficient rest, ingesting a balanced weight-reduction plan, and remaining truely dynamic.

Can Communal Narcissism Be Treated?

Right now, there aren't any FDA-supported treatment options for self-focused person sickness.Five That stated, treatment may be a beneficial, proactive desire for records and adapting to self-centeredness.

Individuals with not unusual selfishness may not at once look for remedy for his or her factor results. They regularly recognize themselves, and it is making an attempt for them to recognize how their methods of behaving or contemplations is probably negative to unique human beings. Some ought to possibly input remedy for assist with unique issues like sorrow, anxiety, substance use, or courting hardships.

If you display conduct predictable with public selfishness and need assistance collectively with your component effects, talk remedy can provide you with a covered spot to red meat up understanding and draw close new adapting competencies. In starting your pursuit, you ought to search for a certified professional with enjoy treating the self-centered behavioral conditions. Consider recording your facet consequences or positioning matters at the Common Self-worried Stock to impart for your expert early this gives each of you a venturing element to start treatment.

Treatment can likewise provide an area of refuge to a person who's handling a common egotist — a specialist can assist making a decision and preserve your limits, and type out whilst and the manner to lessen off a friendship. A net-based completely catalog is an superb approach for getting the whole lot rolling and finding the help you want from an authorized expert.

Current & Further Research on Communal Narcissism

While self-absorption has built up a few ahead momentum as of overdue, shared selfishness is a fairly new time period. At this element, it's far seldom said in fashionable conversations, albeit this will probable change earlier than lengthy.

Individuals with agentic self-absorption and mutual self-absorption every have self-serving goals. However, agentic selfishness zeros in greater on task a wholesome identity development and deference. Individuals with collective selfishness, but, esteem self-improve with the aid of the use of using being prosocial.

Flow studies indicates that people with public self-absorption misjudge and overclaim their shared records. However, there can be no proof assisting their cases. Similarly, meta-examinations show they have even masses much less commonplace facts than humans without collective narcissism.1,6

Further exam is needed on mutual self-centeredness inside the hard work strain, beneficent institutions, and political areas. Since mutual selfishness can be so accursed, preserving on bringing issues to mild of the normal increase word symptoms and signs is pivotal. Moreover, studies on any hybrid affects amongst common selfishness and special emotional properly-being problems is probably treasured.

The Communal Narcissism Inventory

The Mutual Self-centeredness Stock changed into made thru researchers and disbursed thru the American Mental Association. Three A a part of the assertions observe to introduce day problems, and the alternative half applies to destiny contemplations.

Clients should fee on a scale from 1 (firmly deviate) to 7 (unequivocally concur) for the accompanying assertions to rate their degree of mutual self-absorption:

I am the most beneficial individual I apprehend

I am going to deliver peace and justice to the sector.

I am the excellent friend someone might also have.

I can be well known for the satisfactory deeds I need to have completed.

I am (going to be) the first-class determine in the world.

I am the maximum being worried character in my social surrounding.

In the destiny I can be broadly identified for fixing the arena's issues.

I drastically beautify others' lives.

I will deliver freedom to the humans.

I am an terrific listener.

I can be capable of remedy international poverty.

I actually have a completely outstanding have an impact on on others.

I am typically the most expertise person.

I'll make the place a much extra lovely location.

I am distinctly honest.

I may be famous for growing humans's well-being.

Final Thoughts

It's appropriate to feel confused, terrified, or livid if you relate to someone who famous communal narcissism. Although narcissism is a complex illness, it is essential that you bought the assist you want in case you're managing a communal narcissist so you can set up barriers and bypass on in a healthful way. And if you apprehend your self in any of the aforementioned descriptions, receiving the proper care can have a profound effect to your behavior and emotions.

Treatment for Narcissistic Personality Disorder

It is crucial to take have a look at that human beings with this problem seldom are in search of for out remedy. People often start treatment with the encouragement of spouse and kids or to cope with aspect results that final effects from the hassle like despair.

Treatment may be especially trying for individuals with NPD due to the fact they may be often reluctant to recognize the difficulty. This hassle in treatment is typically intensified via the way that coverage groups will more regularly than no longer pay for brief remedy plans that emphasize aspect consequences lower, in place of fundamental person problems.

Some drugs can help with peopling gaining extra noteworthy reviews of their strategies of behaving, laying out a extra intelligible identity, and higher managing their strategies of behaving. These include:

Individual psychodynamic psychotherapy can be successfully used to cope with narcissistic individual sickness, despite the fact that the approach may be possibly hard and extended.

Cognitive behavioral remedy (CBT) is regularly powerful to help humans exchange unfavorable idea and conduct patterns.1 The purpose of remedy is to modify distorted thoughts and create a greater practical self-photo.

Psychotropic medicines are commonly useless for lengthy-term exchange but are every now and then used to cope with signs and signs of hysteria or melancholy.

Coping With Narcissistic Personality Disorder

Individuals who have institutions with a self-absorbed man or woman behavioral state of affairs can also warfare to manipulate their loved one's activities. Individuals with NPD do now not have a lucid identification, so that they frequently take part in hurtful or exploitative ways of behaving which is probably supposed to accumulate attention, regard, or love from others.

Assuming everybody you recognize has NPD, there are some subjects that you can do that could make it more obvious and adapt to their techniques of behaving.

Learn to apprehend narcissistic behaviors. Individuals with NPD can also participate in oppressive sports, for instance, gaslighting that is meant to manipulate others' sentiments and activities. Knowing the manner to understand these ways of behaving is the most important skip closer to handling them all of the extra efficiently.

Put down clean preventing points. Try not to permit the alternative man or woman to coordinate livid, harmful, or outrageous techniques of behaving within the route of you. Put down first rate barriers and uphold them, regardless of whether or not or not it implies slicing off the friendship.

Talk to others. Once in a while, it very well can be hard to understand approaches of behaving which may be oppressive after they have become standardized internal your courting. Having partners, household, or a representative to help you with know-how the elements of your dating assist you to with better figuring out a way to understand whilst the person with NPD has crossed a line.

Encourage the one which you like to are looking for remedy for their state of affairs. Perceive, anyways, that many human beings with NPD by no means look for treatment. On the off hazard that the possibility person may not find out useful resource, remember speaking with a expert or emotional well-being gifted your self. A professional allow you to with attempting to remake self guarantee that has been harmed by way of the use of the connection.

Chapter 5: What Is A Malignant Narcissist? Signs, Causes, & How To Deal With One

A malignant narcissist is a time period used to provide an explanation for someone who has signs and symptoms of every narcissistic character disorder and delinquent character ailment. Combined, those troubles can display up as conceitedness, a need for power and popularity, and inclinations to use or make the most others for selfish reasons.1,2,three Like most character issues, malignant narcissism interferes with relationships and is considered in large component untreatable.2,three,four

What Is a Malignant Narcissist?

Malignant narcissism isn't a proper analysis, however alternatively a commonplace term used to explain a person with dispositions and symptoms and signs of each narcissistic character disorder and antisocial character contamination. Also called pathological narcissists, malignant narcissists commonly generally tend to have extra impairments, worse relationships, and worse responses to treatment than human beings with conventional NPD.2,4

People with narcissistic persona disorder will be predisposed to show off grandiose attitudes, enjoy advanced to others, need excessive praise and validation, and reply very poorly to even the slightest criticism. People with delinquent character sickness lack empathy, dismiss the emotions and goals of others, and use and take advantage of others to fulfill their needs.Five Malignant narcissists tend to display a aggregate of these tendencies and behaviors, which preserve them from forming wholesome relationships.2,three,6

Malignant Narcissists vs. Psychopaths or Sociopaths

Psychopaths and sociopaths are every terms generally used to provide an explanation for humans with antisocial character sickness, however who do no longer show signs and symptoms of narcissistic persona disease (sociopaths and narcissists are pretty unique).1 While each psychopaths and sociopaths show developments of APD, malignant narcissists (furthermore referred to as narcissistic sociopaths) display each narcissistic and delinquent trends, and regularly qualify for a assessment of each APD and NPD.

There is also a mild difference amongst a sociopath and psychopath, in keeping with some researchers who argue psychopaths have a greater immoderate form of antisocial person illness than sociopaths.

The perception is that sociopaths do appear to have a few experience of proper and incorrect, and a few functionality to empathize, making them plenty much less likely to devote dangerous or illegal acts. Psychopaths, as a substitute, aren't believed to have these talents, which means they've got a whole lot less restraint and regularly act aggressively and recklessly.[7]

Traits of Malignant Narcissism

Malignant narcissists display trends and signs of both delinquent and narcissistic man or woman sickness. While every APD and NPD are each varieties of individual problems, the signs and symptoms and trends of each sickness are extraordinary.1,five

The chart under outlines the principle traits and symptoms of every delinquent and narcissistic persona disorders that arise in malignant narcissists:5

Antisocial Traits in Malignant Narcissists

Narcissistic Traits in Malignant Narcissists

A sample of violating the rights of others

Grandiose, smug, or acts advanced

Breaking policies and felony hints

Fantasies about electricity/success/reputation

Deceiving others for delight/private benefit

Needs excessive reward/validation

Impulsive preference making

Feels entitled to crucial treatment

Irritability or aggressiveness

Exploits or makes use of others for non-public advantage

Reckless/risky conduct

Lacking empathy for goals of others

Irresponsibility/loss of capability to feature

Envious of others

Lack of remorse for acts that damage others

Hypersensitive to complaint

Combined, having each antisocial and narcissistic trends has an inclination to motive a very severe shape of pathology.

Malignant narcissists will be predisposed to expose the maximum extreme inclinations of every situations, which may be displayed in the following methods:

Being rather smug and self-centered

Disregarding the emotions and desires of numerous humans

Manipulating, using, or exploiting others for personal advantage or pleasure

Having an immoderate want for electricity

Acts of revenge in competition to folks who criticize them

Fantasizing about strategies to obtain extra electricity or dominance over others

Lacking ethical revel in, regret, or regret for their moves

Being cruel and taking delight within the ache of others

High ranges of aggression in the direction of unique people

Paranoia or distrust of others

What Are the Signs of a Malignant Narcissist?

Threatening egotists will usually show a part of the most instead horrible skills of every APD and NPD, and often have excessive dysfunctions of their connections, art work, and capacity to art work on particular ordinary troubles.

Their silly manner of behaving, dismissal of other humans, and failure to form enduring sound establishments with others could make them lots less tough to come upon than individuals with fewer attributes or less harsh or 'secretive' varieties of selfishness.

The following are 10 signs of a threatening egomaniac:

1. They Use, Misuse, and Dispose of Individuals

One of the critical signs and symptoms of a harmful egomaniac is their prolonged information of utilising, manhandling, and getting rid of people who are as of not useful to them. Individuals nearest to them will regularly see an instance of damaged connections and fellowships, further to own family and soul buddies who've grow to be useless or insignificant to them - regularly after they've implemented them to satisfy a particular diploma of deliver.

2. They Are Fixated on Power

Harmful egotists are frequently starving for electricity and fixated on techniques of getting a greater quantity of it. They frequently strive for occupations that undergo the charge of them this energy, and form establishments with folks which may be inclined enough for them to apply all-out command over. Since they arrive up short of the functionality to find out the energy internal themselves, they've got an outrageous requirement for influential places to inspire them.

three. Everything Is Own for Them

To a unstable egomaniac, everything is private. If a companion or relative pokes amusing at them, neglects to get again to them, or rather on the off hazard that they may be unnoticed for advancement at paintings, they will be profoundly irritated and irate, casting off a self-centered breakdown.

In the egomaniac's truth, there may be no such thing as a guiltless mistakes, oversight, or high-quality explanation for why every person could not cope with them within the manner they count on (and to them, have the proper) to be handled.

four. They Hold Hard emotions and Get Payback

A dangerous egomaniac is handily outraged and at the same time as they may be, their retribution may be cruel. Individuals with this behavioral condition will quite often keep lengthy emotions of spite towards in reality each person who has violated or insulted them in any functionality.

In any occasion, contradicting them, giving them grievance, or addressing some thing they said can bring about short, outrage-stuffed vengeance. They can also rebuff people via erupting, dismissing them, or in any occasion, disposing of them with the aid of and huge.

five. They Take Joy From the Enduring of Others

Threatening egotists may be brutal and, fairly, savage, performing to take a wiped-out delight or fulfillment in the enduring of others. They may possibly laugh or taunt a person who is suffering, purposefully embarrass any individual, or hire man or woman data they have got in opposition to them.

Sadly, this moreover way that they may be hunters who will control, misuse, and take benefit of others, some of the time for the man or woman growth and in a few cases for no precise motive.

6. Nothing Is Ever Their Shortcoming

Egomaniacs (and in particular threatening egotists) commonly do now not assume the fault for any of their phrases or sports activities sports, in any occasion, whilst they're it appears that evidently really off base. All subjects being same, they may quite often erupt, get protecting, and song down techniques of accusing others, in any occasion, when they want to curl and contort reality to do as such.

7. They Are Heartless in Their Quest for What They Need

Harmful egotists will often be savage in their quest for impact, riches, fulfillment, or acknowledgment. At the issue after they need some element, there won't be any line they are reluctant to skip to get it, even on the immediately charge of others they may be saying they care approximately. They would likely lie, control, use, or possibly attack or dishonor others to get what they need.

8. They Don't Have a Still, small voice

An absence of compassion or understand for the feelings and requirements of others is a facet effect of every APD and NPD and is regular in risky egomaniacs. Individuals with this person kind will regularly haven't any regret or lament for topics they've got brought on to damage others.

At times, it very well might be crucial to counterfeit remorse to get what they want, however usually they may concede no horrific conduct with the aid of way of any manner and in fact, do no longer experience lousy for what they've got done.

9. They Have Numerous Foes

It need to wonder no character that a unstable egomaniac should have a significant rundown of foes, which regularly consists of previous partners, darlings, or even humans from their loved ones. Individuals with this behavioral state of affairs will usually make foes successfully and regularly due to the truth to them, even the smallest offense could make them dispose of the complete dating.

Since connections are handiest a critical evil for them, it's in reality smooth for them to sever a tie, irrespective of a person near them.

10. Nobody Will See Their Weaknesses

Where it counts, egotists are very shaky, but a harmful egomaniac may not ever permit those frailties to reveal to precise people. All topics taken into consideration, they will turn out to be careful, blowing up, last down, or in any occasion, obliterating connections when they enjoy compromised or shaky. Likewise, they'll often veil uncertainties inside the again of an outdoor of presumption or pretentiousness.

What Causes Malignant Narcissism?

All emotional well-being troubles, which includes behavioral situations like a whole dismiss for certainly one of a kind humans and self-focused behavioral situations, are ordinary to be introduced about via a mix of each hereditary and ecological elements, in addition to personal temperament.1,2 Some exam has likewise located that there might be a few variations within the wiring and design of the thoughts in people with NPD which assists with making revel in of a part of the element consequences and characteristics of the issues.Three

Some of the non-genetic factors which may be believed to play a causal role in the development of NPD and APD encompass:1,2,three

Encountering misuse or brush aside

Being held to ridiculously precise necessities as a youngster

Being unnecessarily encouraged or scrutinized as a toddler (or each)

Having crabby, psychotic, or forceful person developments

Having a low strain or dissatisfaction resilience

Being excessively delicate and incapable to direct feelings

Being harassed or overlooked in youngsters

Being knowledgeable one is unique or has unusual abilities

Seeing entitled, bombastic, or self-absorbed tendencies in a father or mother

Looking for outer approval or acclaim to make up for low self assurance

Discovering that vulnerable factor is a sign of shortcoming

Discovering that sadness and blend-u.S.A. Of americaare grievous or inadmissible

Extreme spotlight on recognition, acknowledgment, power, and achievement

Absence of mindfulness and inconvenience perceiving feelings in self and others

Disturbed character advancement

How to Deal With a Malignant Narcissist

Sadly, the developments and element outcomes of threatening self-centeredness often straightforwardly have an effect on others, especially those nearest to the person. While coping with an egomaniac, many humans end up survivors of self-absorbed misuse, a specific sort of misuse that often includes manipulate, misdirection, gaslighting, and being exploited.

The consequences of this form of non-prevent maltreatment may be crushing, adversely influencing an character's satisfaction, self warranty, and by the use of way of and large emotional well-being. Frequently, it will become crucial to restriction any association with a damaging egomaniac, specially in the occasion that they have grow to be oppressive or toxic - assuming you're seeing someone's, in all likelihood time to split.

If this isn't always an option, proper right here are some exclusive techniques to address a malignant narcissist to your life:8

Deal along facet your assumptions and do not assume love, reasonableness, or power of mind from them: Threatening egotists are unequipped for legitimate, identical, robust connections

Limit your connections thru keeping cooperation brief, centered, and shallow: This limits your gamble of being damage or taken benefit of through them

Try now not to be excessively helpless or open with them: They might also moreover comprise this individual information as ammo later

Allow them to speak about themselves and be robust: Taking care of their requirement for approval can preserve them once more from utilising forceful strategies

Recognize the strategies they use closer to you (for example acclaim, deceptive friendship, duty, feeling sorry for, and so forth): This allows you understand whilst they'll be making use of them toward you

Comprehend what they want from you and pick out early assuming you can say OK: This keeps up together together with your limits with them, in any occasion, whilst they try and exceed

Comprehend and avoid their triggers/frailties: Causing a self-worried physical difficulty have to make you their aim

Practice looking after oneself and utilize your emotionally supportive community: This safeguards towards the pessimistic intellectual affects of self-absorbed misuse

Can Malignant Narcissism Be Treated?

Malignant narcissists rarely are seeking out remedy or even after they do, their defenses regularly make them proof in opposition to remedy.2,three,4 Honest self-reflected picture that includes treatment often consists of introspection that would uncover flaws, mistakes, and insecurities that malignant narcissists are not able to address.

Still, there are a few exceptions, and people who do are looking for assist for this trouble regularly have some degree of self-focus and additionally a willingness to alternate, which could every make remedy greater effective. The brilliant step to looking for assist for NPD is to reach out to a therapist, and to work on locating a therapist who's informed and experienced in supporting humans with this man or woman illness.

Chapter 6: Eight Steps To Overcoming Your Narcissism

Overcoming narcissism is not any clean system. Absolute change may be close to now not viable. However, you can make changes an fantastic manner to create a extraordinary impact for your life.

Here are eight possible steps that will help you prevent being a narcissist, consistent with psychologists.

1) Know what your "triggers" are

Narcissistic conduct often emerges on the same time as a person receives "added about."

According to Elinor Greenberg, internationally famend Gestalt therapy instructor and Narcissistic Personality Disorder professional:

"triggers" are:

"...conditions, terms, or behaviors that arouse robust bad feelings in you. People with narcissistic issues commonly have a tendency to overreact when they're "caused" and do matters that they later regret."

As a primary step, it's vital to understand in which conditions your narcissism comes out. Learning what they are can help you emerge as aware of the motives in the back of your narcissism, so you may be capable of manage them as a result.

For instance, if you enjoy narcissistic inclinations and need to emerge as aware about your triggers, you may be conscious which you regularly enjoy a surge of anger while someone you understand being of a "lower repute" demanding situations your authority in the place of work.

I consent to receiving emails and customized classified ads.

Or you could phrase which you are regularly dismissive of different human beings after they endorse mind.

Whatever your precise triggers are, start to be aware of them. It may be beneficial to keep a pocket e-book with you or jot them down in a word-taking app for your cell telephone.

Over time, you'll start to word patterns on whilst you experience introduced on by the usage of others and react with narcissistic dispositions.

2) Practice self-love

Narcissistic humans normally generally tend to have important vanity issues and don't recognize the manner to love themselves.

Because in their fragile arrogance, they need to mission their superiority and placed special humans down.

What narcissistic people want to do in particular else is to workout self-love.

But it's no longer clean to practice self-love in recent times. The cause for this is easy:

Society situations us to try to find ourselves in our relationships with others. We're usually searching out "romantic love", "the most effective", or an idealized perception of the "great courting".

When it includes relationships, you might be amazed to concentrate that there's one very crucial connection you've probable been overlooking:

The relationship you've got with yourself.

I observed about this critical insight from the shaman Rudá Iandê.

His outstanding, video on cultivating wholesome relationships, Rudá gives you the tools to plant your self on the center of your global.

And whilst you begin doing that, there's no telling how an awful lot happiness and fulfillment you may discover inside yourself and in your relationships.

So what makes Rudá's advice so existence-changing?

Well, uses techniques derived from the knowledge of shamanic teachings and locations his very personal current-day twist on them. He can be a shaman, but he's skilled the identical issues in love as you and I really have.

And the usage of this combination, he's with out issues recognized the regions wherein most humans bypass incorrect in our relationships.

When you experience like your relationships in no way operating out, or feel undervalued, unappreciated, or unloved, this unfastened video will provide you with some practical and applicable strategies to alternate your love life spherical.

three) Manage your impulses

Narcissist people are frequently impulsive and make alternatives without considering the effects.

If you show narcissist tendencies, it's important to emphasize questioning first and reacting later.

According to Greenberg:

"Practice inhibiting or delaying your regular reaction at the same time as caused. Your 'ordinary' reaction is the now unwanted one which you do routinely. It has become confused as a addiction into the neurons of your brain."

The key step to converting your behaviors is to become aware of your impulses. This gives you the opportunity to create behavioral exchange to your lifestyles.

Taking word of your triggers as recommended in the first step will teach you to create a few location some of the stimulus of the motive and your response.

Pausing while prompted opens up the opportunity to create a present day set of behaviors.

4) Consciously pick a present day set of empathetic responses

It's exceedingly tough for narcissists to don't forget others in advance than thinking about themselves. Although hard, it's a essential step to take.

Research indicates that narcissists can learn how to be empathetic. It comes right right down to growing a addiction out of empathetic behaviors.

Ni advises:

"Express genuine interest in and interest about human beings to your lifestyles. Listen as a minimum as loads as you talk. Be careful now not to thoughtlessly intervene upon others' non-public area, use their non-public assets, or take in their personal time with out permission."

You can begin to teach your self to react differently to situations that cause narcissistic inclinations now which you have become extra aware about your impulses.

Think about the triggers you've been listening to inside the first step, and take some time out to maintain in mind how you would like to react. What would possibly your response be if you had been consciously thinking about others and demonstrating empathy?

It's critical to take some time out and consciously determine at the behaviors you often adopt.

Now which you're taking note of at the same time as you sense delivered about and analyzing to create a area among the stimulus of the motive and your reaction, you can start to consciously react with an empathetic behavior on every occasion you enjoy the reason of narcissism.

It will revel in unusual doing so first of all. It can also be fantastically aggravating. But over time, your new reactions will become ingrained conduct styles.

5) Celebrate the choice you've made to be a higher character

It sounds smooth, however if you have diagnosed your self as having narcissistic tendencies, have began to take note of your impulses and reactions, and have all started to replace your narcissistic reactions with empathic ones, then you definately ought to be very satisfied with yourself.

You have made the choice to grow to be a better model of your self, and also you're following thru with this preference.

It's very vital that this choice is yours and also you're doing it because of the fact you sincerely want to alternate. If that is the case, you want to take a pause to surely rejoice which you've come to this preference. It's now not an clean thing to do.

During the method of creating a modern-day set of behavioral responses to your narcissistic inclinations, I advocate placing apart a tough and rapid time each day for yourself to have amusing the picks you've made.

Think of the moments inside the direction of the day while you located your triggers and substituted your regular reaction with an possibility empathetic conduct. Notice the instances you weren't capable of substitute your response and recognize that it takes time to create a modern-day set of conduct.

By taking time out for yourself each day to have a laugh your self, you'll remind yourself approximately why you're doing what you do. This will provide you with internal motivation to hold your quest to prevent being a narcissist. 6) Take responsibility for the whole lot that takes place on your existence

Narcissists have a recognition for no longer often taking obligation for what occurs in their existence.

They both manipulate the scenario to play the sufferer or make someone else feel accountable for the crime they dedicated themselves.

But now not you. The fact that you've arrived at this thing in the article shows that you are endorsed to begin taking responsibility on your narcissistic inclinations.

This journey of taking duty is some distance large than truely converting a difficult and rapid of narcissistic behavioral dispositions. It might also want to have a miles broader effect in your life.

As Dr. Alex Lickerman explains, taking duty virtually manner:

"...to take whole duty in your happiness ... method recognizing that how subjects take a look at the outset doesn't determine how subjects will end, and that despite the fact that we can't control the whole lot (or probable whatever) we want, all of us have often remarkable ability to influence how an lousy lot happiness or suffering the events of our lives deliver us."

(If you'd like help in taking duty in your life, check out our eBook: Why Taking Responsibility is Key to Being the Best You)

7) Consider taking psychotherapy

Now which you're taking responsibility in your narcissism, it's absolutely worth considering complementing your method to changing your behaviors with psychotherapy.

Taking on practices that can help you to apprehend why you inherently do what you do will help you to recognize your underlying nature in greater intensity.

According to Bridges To Recovery, remedies encompass:

"Working collectively, therapists and narcissistic sufferers will discover the attitudes and behaviors that create stress, warfare, and dissatisfaction inside the affected person's lifestyles. As recovery progresses, therapists will inspire NPD patients to take optimistic motion to ameliorate the negative impact of their narcissistic signs and symptoms and signs and symptoms and signs, imparting realistic advice and education which could help them obtain this."

eight) Practice gratitude

Narcissists frequently have problem records gratitude, as it calls for an entire lot of humility. But this is like a muscle that you may flex and increase.

If there can be one way to quench an inflated ego, practising gratitude will in reality do the trick.

This is because of the fact gratitude shifts you from thinking about yourself to feeling grateful for other people and topics to your life.

John Amadeo, award-triumphing writer of Dancing with Fire: A Mindful Way to Loving Relationships, explains:

"Gratitude is a corrective to our sense of entitlement. One factor of narcissism is the perception that we need to get even as now not having to offer. We enjoy that we're entitled to fulfill our dreams without being stricken with the useful resource of perceiving a few different's worldwide and responding to others' dreams. Our interest is truly absorbed internal a restrained and slim sense of self."

But how will you nearly start education gratitude while you understand your narcissistic personality doesn't permit you do to so?

Begin with yourself.

I recognize it would confuse you but right proper right here's the component:

You don't want to look for outdoor fixes to type out your life, deep down, you understand this isn't running.

And that's because of the reality till you appearance inside and unharness your private electricity, you'll in no way locate the pride and success you're searching for.

This is some one of a kind hassle I found from the shaman Rudá Iandê. In his amazing unfastened video, Rudá explains powerful techniques to collect what you want in existence. And I'm first-rate it's going to moreover permit you to examine practical processes to exercising gratitude and conquer your narcissism.

So, in case you want to get maintain of authentic recommendation about building a healthful dating with your self, don't hesitate to observe his notable masterclass.

Negative Impacts Of Narcissism

Tragically, human beings experiencing self-centeredness can almost be altogether ignorant about their negative manner of behaving and the effect it welcomes on their lives.

As consistent with Teacher Preston Ni, life mentor, and creator of How to Convey Really and Handle Troublesome Individuals:

"Numerous egotists are absent to their horrible and regularly useless requirements of conduct, which typically result in them encountering life examples the maximum tough manner viable."

The bad results of self-centeredness on your life can embody:

1) Depression and segregation

Egotistical conduct inclinations like childishness, untruths, and unresponsiveness are not attributes that appeal to long lasting connections.

Egomaniacs are often crammed to serve actually themselves and are unequipped for depicting compassion in the course of others. Along the ones strains, they experience problem shaping licensed and profound bonds with others.

As indicated with the useful useful resource of professional Award Hilary Brenner:

"The need to do that self-smart hard exercise to preserve an air pocket of self perception is depleting on oneself in addition to specific humans, continuously taking steps to find a crude nerve, and the use of numerous crucial connections into horrendous forms of jealousy and contest, or poverty and misuse, in outrageous however definitely pretty regular events."

This implies egotists maintain on with forlorn lives and may preserve up with shallow connections.

2) Issues in vocation or college

Normally, an egomaniac's social uncouthness represses them from winning inside the profession or instructive stepping stool.

As in step with Ni, issues emerge from:

"... rule-breaking, gross flippancy, inconsiderate extravagance, or one-of-a-kind careless activities."

At the stop of the day, egomaniacs arise quick on the ability to excel at the vocation stepping stool.

3) Superfluous annoyance

Outrage is a few aspect egotistical humans will usually cultivate.

As indicated thru Greenberg:

"They lash out at things that look like very minor to the large majority, including sitting tight an extra ten mins for a desk in a café.

Their level of rage and damage will seem like quite unbalanced to the actual condition."

This vital pessimistic inclination cuts down each part of an egomaniac's existence, making it appreciably more tough for them to perform pride or bliss.

4) Gloom and tension

Egotists are not by using the usage of way of any stretch of the creativeness effective to inner profound contentions. A tremendous contrary, they're greater sensitive to despondency and anxiety.

Yale research expert Seth Rosenthal makes enjoy of this: "What human beings speculate is that egomaniacs are inclined to higher upsides and worse low elements. They have this normal want to have their significance showed by using manner in their popular environment. At the factor whilst reality well-knownshows them, they may reply via manner of the use of becoming discouraged."

The issue that topics is, that they employ their battles as fuel for the detestable manner of behaving, similarly estranging themselves from the sector.

5) Well-established uncertainty

Individuals experiencing Self-centered Behavioral conditions may additionally seem like careless, but in the back of their shells is any man or woman who's affected by firmly mounted susceptible aspect.

As indicated via Ni:

"Numerous egotists are successfully angry with a-the big apple proper or visible affronts or obliviousness. They are typically with the useful aid of the weak point that individuals may not see them because the advantaged, strong, famous, or "extremely good" human beings they make themselves to be.

"Where it counts, severa egotists sense much like the "atypical one out", regardless of whether or now not they agonizingly have no preference to honestly allow it out."

Could an egomaniac at any detail simply alternate?

Indeed.

However, there is a number one if.

As in line with ensured mentor and improvement idea pioneer Barrie Davenport: "If an egotist's social examples may be changed in treatment, it could help with diminishing their unbendable self-focused developments proper right into a milder form of self-safety that at closing permits them to have solid connections."

Change is plausible with progressing endeavors. If you are to be had to roll out profound enhancements to your mind-set and the way you maintain on collectively along side your life, you can defeat your self-absorbed propensities and feature a advanced relationship with the vicinity.

Refusal is the principle instance you want to interrupt.

The awesome way to push earlier is to renowned that you have an trouble, get a experience of possession with it, and be to be had to change.

How this one revelation changed my narcissistic life

I used to certainly take transport of I need to had been fruitful earlier than I had the right to find out any individual who may moreover need to cherish me.

I used to in reality take delivery of there has been a "fantastic person" available and I honestly needed to tune down them.

I used to definitely accept I could at extended remaining be pleased as quickly as I determined "the one".

What I can't deny is that the ones limiting convictions had been preventing me from building profound and personal connections with people I end up assembly. I grow to be pursuing a deception that changed into using me to forlornness.

If you've got had been given any choice to transform some issue on your life, one of the excellent methods is to exchange your convictions.

Sadly, it's miles some factor however some factor easy to do.

I'm fortunate to have worked straightforwardly with the shaman Rudá Iandê in converting my convictions approximately affection. Doing so has in a vast feel changed my existence for eternity.

Perhaps the maximum high-quality video we have were given is on his experiences with affection and closeness. Rudá Iandê separates his essential illustrations on growing sturdy and assisting connections on your each day life.

Love is some thing we need to chip away at interior ourselves, no longer some detail that we anticipate or take from each extraordinary individual...

The more we are capable of begin to analyze and cherish the quantities of ourselves that we want to run from and exchange, the more we will truly and extensively well known who we're as people.

Now that you are greater prepared to test whether or not or not or not you have self-focused characteristics, you've got were given the selection to move in, accomplish the work, and begin to roll out a long lasting development for your self.

It's no longer commonly smooth to alternate. However, it's miles an excursion that you do now not need to do by myself. As you run over more belongings and mind for this change, actually make sure that some thing comes from the profound inner and a few component that focuses you lower once more into your self.

Essentially taking the exhortation of others will pass over the mark to your ears.

Getting into your coronary coronary coronary heart and profound quintessence, it's far a way that no person but you could look at. Recall that the apparatuses and property that assist you with doing this may be the fine for your excursion.

I want you fortitude and strength en path.

Chapter 7: How To Be Less Controlling

Maintaining your personal feeling of well-being similarly in your interpersonal and professional connections relies upon on studying the way to save you being domineering. You are organized to begin the way of letting pass of control when you have previously found out which you show controlling conduct. Although it takes guts and perseverance to discover ways to permit skip, the pride you can experience when you do is properly really worth the try.

Shift your hobby to what you could manipulate: your existence

1. DECIDE THE FOUNDATION OF YOUR REQUIREMENT FOR CONTROL.

You need to apprehend the hidden reasons for manipulate to discern out the way to emerge as lots less controlling. The requirement for manage is attached to our Six Human Necessities, which can be the important thing requirements that manual our picks as an entire and contemplations. Controlling way of behaving is once in a while persuaded through the usage of the usage of necessities: importance and guarantee. We have a actual enjoy of reassurance and safety whilst we're positive due to the fact we understand what is in hold. We enjoy love and want thru importance.

We discern out a way to satisfy these cravings via unlucky techniques, for instance, the want to use command over the entirety round us, on the equal time as they may be no longer tended to in strong techniques. These strategies may additionally have all of the earmarks of being feasible for a while for the motive that they deliver the presence of safety. In any case, they might smash our connections and allow us to enjoy more be and uncertain than at any time in contemporary memory.

Control over your viewpoints

2. ASSEMBLE YOUR MINDFULNESS

You'll begin to recognize what your requirement for control method for others in addition to yourself after you deal with its hidden reasons. You need to don't forget that being controlling is useful, yet in fact, it without a doubt leaves humans considering a way to conform to controlling humans, much like you. It's massive to pause for a minute and recall whether or no longer or not your endeavors to exercise manage are having a protracted lasting effect.

Ponder calling your jobless sister every week to watch out for her improvement closer to getting some artwork. Rather than deciding on the week after prone telephone alternatives, do not forget whether you're blocking your sister's pursuit of employment. Continue to name assuming the response is confirmed (and your sister values the week-after-week calls). Quit calling at the off hazard which you get a no. You might also attract with human beings and with your self all of the more delicately thru being more aware of your lead.

3. REINVENT YOUR PSYCHE

Tony's critical conviction is that you may transform your thoughts to have an effect on how your propensities are communicated. Permitting bypass of manage calls for studying the proscribing thoughts which may be impacting your manner of behaving in region of letting your unexamined mind-set anticipate command. Be aware about your thoughts and remember whether they will be useful to you.

Pause for a minute to evaluate the scenario the following time you have have been given anxiety or view your self thinking about how as much less controlled. Who or what are you alarmed via? What is it approximately this case that makes me uncomfortable? Consider your inquiries as an unconditional meeting to generate new thoughts wherein you aren't condemning any mind that strike a chord. Be sincere and touchy with yourself. As you figure out a way to be cautious about your viewpoints and responses, you can become extra aware, so as to help you in letting with going of manipulate.

4. RESTRICT CONTROL-ARRANGED LANGUAGE FROM YOUR JARGON

At the component whilst you exchange your terms, you remodel your self. Figuring out a way to be an entire lot a whole lot less controlling requires perceiving the undertaking of language. Figure out the manner to understand the language you operate to exercise manipulate - as an instance, framing casual comments in innocent language (like "have you ever at any component taken into consideration… ") or scrutinizing a partner's attitude on a few random situation.

You'll likewise have to change your interior self-communicate. What is your inner speech speaking approximately while you experience the requirement for manage? At the detail at the same time as you recognize your horrific self-speak, you may supplant them with attractive ones, shift your outlook and manage your uneasiness - and your requirement for manage. Rather than emotional concerns approximately lousy topics taking area, ask yourself how practical your feelings of trepidation are. Would may additionally need to head incorrect? Figure out a manner to be lots less controlling via halting yourself before it even starts offevolved offevolved.

human beings managed

5. FOSTER YOUR RELATIONAL ABILITIES

The trouble of the manner to give up being an obsessive-compulsive character is not direct all of the time. You would possibly probable manage the two those who need some diploma of control (like your youngsters, your understudies, or your people) and the individuals who consider you need to ease off (like your accomplice and pals). This state of affairs can location you in a clumsy nook, but, the key's correspondence.

The requirement for manipulate can eliminate our capability to interface with others on the identical time as what we want to do is boom sympathy and the functionality to apprehend people on a profound degree. Pay hobby for your accomplice's necessities. Ask your pals how you can get to the subsequent stage. Surrender a hint of manipulate together along with your kids. The requirement for control does now not need to damage connections.

6. TAKE ON BETTER PROPENSITIES

Solid propensities like contemplation, guidance, and perception can assist you with facilitating anxiety, middle your power, and allow you a vicinity to respire to chip away on the way to not be controlling. Taking care of oneself is some extraordinary essential exercise on the off chance that you want manage. Make getting a few downtime part of your regular each day exercising, and you may see second blessings out of your angle.

You can likewise contain your requirement for improvement that will help you with identifying a way to stop being controlling. Feed your brain with books about a manner to now not be controlling or talk with a expert. As you switch out to be extra knowledgeable, you'll be better ready to apprehend your behaving negative strategies of behaving and supplant them with better ones.

7. GET AN EXTERNAL VIEWPOINT

Rather than shifting towards relinquishing control through your restricted endeavors, be a part of up with the help of a confided-in associate or professional. Pick someone with whom you've got were given number one regions of power, and request their contribution on manners through that you are being managed. By getting an external component of view, you're prepared to differentiate and trade oblivious techniques of behaving originating out of your compulsiveness.

Request that normal companions draw the ones approaches of behaving out into the open as they emerge. Perceive that, at the equal time as it thoroughly can be appealing to provide others steering, the most wonderful manner to adore any individual is virtually, and which means ceasing from endeavoring to trade them.

Over the long haul, you may start to see that on the off danger that you do not parent out a manner to end being controlling, your endeavors at manipulate will begin to manipulate you. You need to decide out the way to relinquish the beyond so it quits inflicting uneasiness in the present. You have zero control over the whole lot, except you have got got a few manage over your demeanor and way to cope with life.

Chapter 8: Real Life Truth About Selfishness

How regularly in that you in a state of affairs at the same time as you favored to withdraw or near your self from supporting others? How regularly have you not noted the wishes and feelings of others due to the fact you have got been considering your self and your interests?

I had my first taste of this as a growing teenager inside the community. Often, I modified into invited to play at the streets with pals. It have become in reality amusing to be inside the commercial business enterprise organisation of satisfied and unfastened-energetic youngsters like me. But one manner or the opposite on the same time as playing those video games some form of fireplace sparked within me that desired me to be on pinnacle of everybody else. I constantly desired to win. It didn't rely who were given harm with the techniques I planned, as long as, I received the game. So hundreds so that in a simple enterprise like cover and are searching out, dishonest will be inevitable for any teen.

As a scholar, the aggressive power in every and each pupil to be the nice became really lingering. At first, I concept I only favored to research and pass my subjects. Then I positioned that being on top mattered to this society. I located that A pupil's constantly had a totally specific place in school. Most importantly, they have been cherished via their mother and father and instructors. The unconscious me changed into decided to be on pinnacle. From the child who honestly desired to be on pinnacle, I started out to be the adolescent who labored tough to be on top and to stay on pinnacle. So I did. I actually have turn out to be a quick learner who refused to teach and help the gradual ones. I were given the A's and that they had been given the C's and the lowly F's. I deserved the A. They deserved the F. It have become a honest endeavor or so I belief.

At work, there were numerous instances after I refused to help officemates over a undertaking they were attempting their great to remedy but might have been without trouble performed had I helped or taught them. That's actually the way it is. Some people find out duties extra hard than others. Unfortunately, the "boss" ought to be around to look or as a minimum want to understand that I made all of it feasible. I deserve a advertising and marketing and advertising over absolutely everyone else. I deserve a higher revenue than anybody else. I recall I turn out to be higher than lots of my colleagues.

Looking returned, I want to confess than I had been selfish myself in extra procedures than one.

In families, controversy typically arrives in swarms of dire. For instance, I even have witnessed relationships shattered due to the reality the ones who have greater without a doubt denied people who have been in financial catastrophe. I clearly have visible sturdy members of families fail to attain out to weaker contributors for the duration of instances of sorrow. It's very smooth to discover a motive out. We have our private issues and problems. I am as broke, as forced, as scared, as you are. More divisive troubles upward thrust up with reference to who receives extra on the same time as a family member dies. Suddenly, every body receives worried. The egocentric desire or what we aptly call greed surfaces. Family contributors hire the dirtiest of way and strategies forgetting they're hurting their personal individuals of the family and blood.

In my suburb, we had a neighbor who in no way joined any birthday celebration inside the network. No depend how oftentimes the circle of relatives became invited, they surely wouldn't come. Until I left domestic for big opportunities in the large city, I by no means observed them be part of gatherings. The family ought to constantly agenda an out-of-town enjoy at some stage in holidays. They were the richest inside the suburb. It modified into unusual that they were in no manner round in any of our a laugh-stuffed events. Later we decided out that their refusal to join our gatherings changed into due to their notion that they may be giving more than what they need to get keep of. They might rather spend their difficult earned coins for circle of relatives journeys than squander it to strangers.

Let's face it. We can be egocentric. There is in each people the tendency to be selfish. It is through our very nature to position ourselves and our pursuits first. It is flawlessly herbal to aspire for what is extremely good for us. The tendency to recall ourselves first and placed our interests above the relaxation is rightly human. It is within the very law of natural desire that we guard our very own that lets in you to live in this loopy worldwide we live in.

However, it's a one-of-a-kind tale while these tendencies grow to be constantly first-rate mother and father and we brush aside others. We need to be careful if we're or have come to be self-absorbed and self-focused maximum vital us to undermine our worthwhile relationships with others.

Selfishness can be synonymous to being self-serving, self-targeted, self-absorbed, self-focused, self-critical, self-absorbed, self-possessed, self-indulgent, self-engrossed or self-disturbing. It's regularly approximately me, myself and I. You and others do now not matter wide variety. We make ourselves the very last reference on the subject of other human beings and conditions. Our want and desires are often the maximum crucial making us inconsiderate and rude, uncaring and stressful, greedy and manipulative.

Selfishness isn't always in reality about what we do, like inside the case of my neighbor who intentionally refuses attending village activities for worry that they can be giving greater than what they must get maintain of. Selfishness is also what we do not do, like depending on the street sweeper to smooth up the muddle on the equal time as we have to have with out troubles picked it up ourselves however selected to overlook about it.

Selfishness is a loss of attitude. It is a manifestation of our fears and a signal of our susceptible point. We pick out out to withhold our time, competencies or treasure for fear of the consequences at the manner to simplest help boom the pursuits of others rather than ourselves. The fast learner in college hesitates to expose the sluggish learner for worry that a person else gets an A except him. Colleagues at artwork are reluctant to mentor each unique for fear someone else except them receives the credit score rating score. On a deeper level, we withhold forgiveness for fear of being harm once more. Everything boils all the way all the way right down to me, myself and I.

Worse, on this crazy international of selfishness is greed and manipulation at paintings. What is mine is mine. What is yours can be mine. Selfish human beings are determined at getting "what they need, when they want it," the least bit price, irrespective of who gets harm. Selfish people are inconsiderate of what others need, suppose and sense. Selfish human beings commonly want to be on pinnacle of factors and in a subtle way ought to lease techniques to govern people and conditions.

Chapter 9: Dealing With Selfishness

How do I apprehend if I am egocentric? Am I even conscious I am egocentric? How do I realize that what I in reality have are selfish tendencies which are rightly natural? How do I recognize I am simply egocentric?

It is tough for a selfish man or woman to peer his or her egocentric side. It is hard for someone who is self-focused, self-absorbed, self-engrossed, self-targeted, self-irritating and self-righteous to be aware she or he is genuinely selfish. You cannot make the blind see what's glaringly seen.

Question is, is it possible for someone selfish to realize they're selfish? Answer is, is it feasible for a blind character to appearance another time? If your answer is yes and it's miles feasible for the blind to see once more, making a person see his egocentric side is feasible as properly.

If your solution isn't always any, I may suggest you prevent studying this e-book. I guarantee you that it is a pointless workout to continue with the succeeding chapters if you find out it not possible for selfish people to apprehend their egocentric difficulty. In the equal way that it's miles ironic for someone to reap remedy at the same time as the sickness has not been recognized. The physician can not prescribe any treatment to a patient except he is aware about what wishes to be healed. For recuperation to come back approximately, the affected man or woman must apprehend what his infection is and be willing to go through remedy.

As a warning, I truly have to inform you that the way of uncovering the selfishness in you'll be inconvenient. You need to open your self as plenty due to the fact the possibility of having harm. Any scientific way to facilitate recovery can be inconvenient or may hurt.

Matter of reality, fact hurts. Are you organized?

Chapter 10: The Selfish Me Uncovered

This e-book is unique because not like many precise mental or inspirational books, it essentially avoids preaching or essentially discussing the difficulty available. Here, you get involved in the method. You are this ebook's co-creator. You will think and you may want to make selections. You will decipher and you could need to take movements.

Let's start with some questions which you need to answer yourself and some conditions that could take place to you in actual life. What selections will you are making?

Situation #1. You are scheduled to education consultation at a gymnasium together along with your instructor to shed those more pounds, all at once a near friend calls and badly dreams your help. You...

1. Go out your manner to assist your pal and indefinitely do away with your appointment together with your gym teacher.

2. You visit your buddy and depart absolutely in time in your gymnasium appointment.

3. Lie and make all kinds of excuse such as you are not feeling well and continue together together with your appointment. You badly want to shed off the ones extra kilos.

If you visit your buddy and depart truly in time to your gym appointment, you're bordering selfishness. There is that this little show of problem. If you pick to lie and make all styles of excuse, you're virtually selfish. You come to be so preoccupied along with your very own issue of losing the ones extra pounds; virtually disregarding your pal who badly needed you at their time of need.

Situation #2. You do not agree of your companion's new experience of favor. It doesn't healthful your flavor. You…

1. You inform your accomplice you could't stand this new revel in of favor and make derogatory remarks. You continuously understand excellent.

2. You specific your private opinion but will understand his sense of style. It may work out.

three. You receive your partner's experience of style and it doesn't in fact problem you even in case you find it horrible. It's his very personal style and way of expressing himself.

You are actually egocentric even as you count on you generally apprehend amazing. You see your self as continuously proper and your accomplice is incorrect. So you figure your way to persuade him to ensure you have got it your manner and get what you want. You go to the quantity of making threats if your companion appears not to understand your aspect. You are obsessed on the concept that your associate surely does not understand what she or he is into. As a devoted lover, you argue that he looks terrible. Come on. It's absolutely style and a manner of expressing themselves. It acquired't harm you. Let flow and don't be so self-targeted.

Situation #3. You owe the financial institution cash after figuring out from one economic catastrophe to another and your dad and mom willingly volunteered to help you pay the monthly expenses. All of the unexpected, you get a hobby and part of your profits is sufficient to pay half of of what you pay the economic corporation monthly. You...

1. Tell your parents approximately your new interest and volunteer to pay half of of of the monthly expenses. You understand that your dad and mom want to experience their tough earned cash and recognize that they have been extra than willing that will help you through your financial issues.

2. Tell your parents approximately your new approach and earnings however request them to keep paying so you are capable of preserve till you may emerge as more financially independent.

3. Do not inform your parents about your new task and earnings. You cause to your self that your mother and father have extra money than you.

If you pick out now not to tell your mother and father approximately your new gadget and income, you are egocentric. We can't make our incapacities or shortcomings a lame excuse no longer to offer or percent. You have grow to be too self-demanding of your very personal problems without considering how inconvenient it have come to be for others to help you within the first location and however they decided on to. Perhaps, you determined that during this situation your mother and father are not ready as a way to help and that they certainly understand your scenario. You have grow to be too fixated along facet your very personal wishes.

Situation #four. You noticed on television that human beings tormented by a modern-day typhoon need help. You certainly have to be had cash and sources but you have got been looking to shop for a extremely-modern pair of footwear the usage of that economic financial savings. You….

1. Proceed to buy those new pair of footwear and persuade yourself that there may be plenty help coming in from anywhere.You speak yourself into believing that your contribution is insignificant besides.

2. You donate half of of of what you stored and placed on preserve what you've got been trying to shop for. You can keep saving and

buy the ones new pair of shoes at a later time.

3. You donate your whole economic economic savings and forget approximately the ones new pair of shoes. It isn't as important as the ones people tormented by the brand new hurricane.

If you make bear in mind that your contribution is insignificant, that there are other human beings inclined to assist and also you maintain to shop for what you want however the suffering round you, you're honestly selfish. You do not care in any respect. People and instances round you do no longer depend. All that topics is you, your wishes and your desires. Situations like this frequently supply out the herbal generosity in us. If materialism is the deliver for selfishness then the diploma of such is actually alarming.

Situation #5. You have been trying to have a baby and feature long gone via quite some clinical treatments. You found your buddies are going to have a infant. You...

1. Are happy for them. You proper away name your pals to congratulate them and time table a visit so you can deliver your offers for their approximately-to-be-born infant.

2. Are green with envy of your pals however deliver them a thoughtful take a look at to allow them to recognize how satisfied you're for them.

3. Are mad and decide to keep away from them even as you may. You determine to hang around extra regularly with buddies who have no children.

It is comprehensible to revel in unhappy if you have lengthy preferred some element and it despite the fact that hasn't came about. It is hectic on the identical time as you discover that it's far a whole lot much less tough for others to have what you have got got preferred with tons much less try or no try at all. You have the proper to enjoy unhappy, but failing to have fun the fun and triumphs of others is selfish. Feeling resentment against your friends who're going to have a infant and finding out to avoid them is genuinely selfish.

Situation #6. Your agency treats its top employees with a bonus vacation journey and you are considered one in every of them. Everybody desires to go to an island wherein the beaches are majestic. Being the most travelled, you insist which you've been to the brilliant of all majestic seashores. They do now not agree and also you misplaced an trouble. You...

1. Willingly conform to what the rest of the institution dreams. In times like this, it isn't the terrific of places but the exquisite of pals that makes a holiday journey honestly amusing.

2. Try tougher to convince your colleagues however recognize their choice in the long run and be a part of the enterprise organisation day experience.

3. Withdraw from the holiday and request your boss to offer your percentage so that you can go to the incredible region . You comprehend very well that they made the incorrect desire.

Unfortunately, you continually want it your manner. So, what in case you are the most traveled and the most knowledgeable of the first rate places in town? So, what if they're not as travelled as you, and in all likelihood for a few that is their first commercial enterprise business enterprise revel in? Withdrawing from the company day out because you accept as true with you studied they're all incorrect suggests how lots of a spoiled brat you're. You are sincerely egocentric. You have to now not even undergo in mind what the entire institution dreams. It is normally what you want and assuming you constantly recognize high-quality. You are selfish because of the fact you forget what will make others happy. Instead, you sulk, you withdraw and bypass your private manner.

Situation #7. Your mom has to juggle time from work, household chores and favors from human beings of the circle of relatives. She has been careworn out for days and has ultimate dates to satisfy with clients. She asks you to help out with the own family chores. This isn't always your kind of stuff. You…

1. Make masses of excuses and pretend you are busy with something else to avoid family responsibilities. You skip on along with your personal commercial enterprise and hardly ever care how stressed your mom is.

2. Offer a bit help but high-quality the ones which you find out handy.

three. Go from your manner to assist your mom although this indicates a touch sacrifice from you to ease her burden of juggling time from art work, family chores and favors from circle of relatives participants.

If you spot your mother's anxiety over dozens of obligations that want to be completed and also you in no manner offer help if you have all the time in the international, you are selfish. I recognize you hate family chores otherwise you indulge in what is convenient and detest what is not. If you select to live indoors your comfort area unmindful of the way you may have eased your mother's load whilst she needed you. You are egocentric.

Situation #eight. You and your sibling percent one room. He or she informs you that a chum is coming for a sleepover. You do no longer similar to the idea of a stranger invading the privacy of your room. You...

1. Allow your brother's friend to live for the night time time. It's actually one night time time besides and you'll make him happy. You can recover from one night time of inconvenience.

2. Agree with the sleep over however you cross find every other place wherein you can spend the night without all of us annoying you.

3. Tell your brother that a sleepover isn't feasible as long as you percentage one room. Your privateness is the most essential among some various things.

It is idea that privateness is a proper of anyone. Understand that it is excellent one night time of inconvenience with a purpose to make your brother the happiest individual in the world. A night time of sacrifice wouldn't harm you. There will certainly be days at the same time as you'll need your brother to do the identical choose out for you. You are downright egocentric to disclaim your brother that small choice. Let pass. Often, a touch giving may be a brilliant feeling.

Situation #nine. It is your father's birthday and he requests if you can go and watch a film together. You've been very busy these days however it isn't always very frequently that your father makes those small requests. You...

1. Explain on your father which you are really so tied up with artwork and can't manage to pay for to move see a movie with him. You inform him you could allow him realize as soon as you are free out of your busy time table.

2. You ask someone else to go out on a film date with him to his preferred film in his favored theater.

3. Go to the films together with your father. It is his birthday.

Come on. You do no longer even must assume twice. It's your vintage guy's birthday. Although he's now not been very outspoken and open approximately it, your dad misses you. Remember the ones many nights he would in all likelihood take you on a film date irrespective of such a lot of responsibilities that he desired to complete? Don't be selfish. Go, buy the ones tickets and don't make any excuses. It's going to be a laugh for you and your dad. t's going to be an extremely good birthday for him.

Situation #10. You all at once bumped into genuinely considered one of your early life friends whom you haven't visible for a long time. You each get excited and speak about the manner you've been. You...

1. Are keen and involved to concentrate and recognise how your friend has been doing.

2. Are excited to concentrate for your friend's recollections and moreover satisfied to percent your non-public recollections as well.

3. Manipulate the verbal exchange and also you typically have a tendency to cognizance on what's taking area on your existence. You every so often listen to your friend.

I like to spend a lot time speaking approximately myself. I am very pleased with my modern repute and accomplishments. Selfish human beings are with out issues intimidated even as someone else receives the center stage because they generally want it for themselves. I am the incredible. I continuously want to be the incredible. I normally need extraordinary humans's approval. I crave for others interest. Share the pride of different humans's achievement. Take word that you do no longer have the monopoly of the place's right subjects in life.

Chapter 11: Looking Closer On The Selfish Me

What did you experience on the equal time as answering the ones questions? How did you fare? Have you uncovered the egocentric you? Do you apprehend of humans spherical you - inside your circle of relatives, among your circle of friends, to your network who display off those symptoms and signs of selfishness? How does this make you experience?

One of the most crucial questions surrounding our necessities of behavior is, "why can't one be selfish", "why must one be now not egocentric". From the moment we start interacting with others, we are taught to proportion our food, our toys and permit others to have the primary slice of cake or the privilege to pick out which element he needs at the same time as you're the one dividing. Most often, we are taught to act in choice of the alternative's interest over our personal.

Funny, but you start asking that isn't it herbal for the inner us to defend our private wants and needs earlier than we are capable of understand the need and dreams of others? As said, at the start of this ebook on this loopy international, it's far perfectly regular and naturally proper to get ahead of others.

Historically, there have been 3 methods of drawing close selfishness. They range from self-upkeep to acts of altruism. If we're privy to them, then it is maximum probably that we're able to keep away from or prevent being egocentric.

The first , of which we are involved with is self-renovation. First, to cause out that there may be nothing incorrect with being egocentric ultimately. Second, it's far one's non-public interest not to be egocentric. The 0.33 one that promotes altruism offers balancing one's private interest and the interest of others.

I want to remind you although that there can be a pleasing line separating what may be egocentric and no longer selfish. Also, no longer all giving is synonymous to generosity. When the giving expects some issue in go back or there's even the slightest interest to advantage from it, that is selfishness. For giving to be actual and altruistic, is continuously geared at the advantage and interest of others and none for yourself. If we're privy to that, then we are able to keep away from or stop being egocentric.

Chapter 12: Understanding Selfishness

Selfishness is born out of worry. We have our personal dreams, dreams and plans. Many oldsters are scared that we may not realize them if we start beginning ourselves and allow others to percentage with our "meager" property.

By the way, meager may be relative. We may have extra than what we need however usually locate ourselves attempting. Nothing is sufficient for us. Nothing satisfies us.

Remember our example of the egocentric son or daughter who refuses to inform their mother and father of their new mission and earnings in order that they gained't be obliged to pay for the other 1/2 in their month-to-month financial institution charges even though they are able to have enough money to? They can justify this with the aid of explaining that their mother and father have extra cash. They in addition defend their moves through pronouncing that they want to store until they might come to be more financially robust. What approximately the son or daughter's mother and father? Aren't they presupposed to enjoy their difficult earn coins? Yet they decided on to assist the son or daughter this is going through economic trouble? They may need to have effects argued that it's miles no longer their duty to bail them out.

Do we now not sometimes find out ourselves inside the same state of affairs? Have we been so preoccupied with our goals that we neglect approximately the wishes of others? Have we been so possessed thru our dreams that we neglect about that one-of-a-type human beings moreover have goals? Have we become so disturbing with our private issues that we omit out on the problems of others.

In this loopy, crazy international, we have emerge as so scared of losing control, of being left at the back of, of no longer being at the bandwagon, so we discover ways to withdraw. We near our doorways. We intentionally create plans and techniques to be on pinnacle and to stay on top. We have become selfish.

You have end up selfish, I need you to be aware about that. In the equal manner every person compete for our spot on this worldwide, is a matter of perspective in place of a reality, and so is selfishness. You have turn out to be selfish. You by using using manner of nature ought to be beneficiant and so must the sector you live in.

You want to be questioning, you're kidding proper? How can you contradict your very very own announcement? You in reality stated at the start of this ebook that we can be selfish and it's miles through manner of our very nature to place ourselves and our pastimes first? Now you tell me that it's far with the useful resource of our very nature to be beneficiant. Are you playing video video games with me? You have to be kidding.

I want you presently to stop, look and concentrate. I am not playing video video video games with you, you are right. It is with the resource of our very nature to place ourselves and our hobbies first, that's a fundamental instinctual need. You need to love your self first in advance than you can love others. However, loving your self first does no longer suggest you need to prevent loving others. Taking care of your desires first does now not endorse you need to prevent being concerned for others. Putting your interests first does no longer imply you want to brush aside the pastimes of others.

Chapter 13: Characteristics Of Selfishness

Characteristic # 1. Selfishness is a made of lack of confidence. Lack of arrogance is a trait apparent in selfish humans. They often are disapproving of others and awful in the direction of life in vast. Their horrible mind-set toward existence and others makes them awful company players. They normally have unpleasant comments toward others, they commonly typically have a tendency to disagree with others evaluations and tips, they'll be regularly important of others even without basis in any respect.

They can't allow pass of their failures and hurts within the beyond and they reflect this on others. They put on mask and pretend that they're on pinnacle of things. They positioned others down for personal benefit. They find it difficult to encourage others due to the fact they themselves do no longer trust that existence is ideal and there is a stunning international reachable. This can also appear very cruel, but a whole lot of the time the selfish person does not realize what they will be virtually doing to others.

Characteristic # 2. Selfishness fears consider. Selfish people are scared of taking off themselves as plenty as others and they devise walls as a defense mechanism. Sometimes they will be rarely into long lasting and massive relationships with others. The pals they do have they determine on to control. The tendency to govern creates a whole lot of troubles due to the truth nobody wants to be within the organization enterprise of or in a dating with a controlling character.

Selfish human beings with this feature see and pay attention handiest themselves. Their tendency to distrust makes them uninvolved and uncaring in a dating. They are so centered with themselves and usually want it their way. They are very possessive of what they non-public and are suspicious of others movements of wanting to harm them.

Characteristic # 3. Selfishness harbors situations. "Quid pro quo, sil vous plait"due to the fact the French would say it. If you want some thing from me then you have to deliver a few factor in skip again. Selfish humans make an account for the whole thing they deliver. They are tremendous at amassing and calculating. They will be predisposed to keep matters for themselves. They'd pick out out to look their amassed property go to waste instead of percent them with others. If they determine to percentage, they could subtly name for some thing in pass returned or would really like for others to take be privy to their "generosity". Altruism or sacrifice is in no way a part of their vocabulary. They never apprehend the pride of giving.

Characteristic # 4. Selfishness nurtures deceit and manipulation. This characteristic comes from the egocentric preference of usually trying to win and to be on pinnacle of anyone else. "I am the high-quality, I am the boss, I am invincible." They have a big ego and are generally looking to be on pinnacle of things and go away no room for other's reviews, suggestions, want and goals. They take offense whilst humans do now not behave everyday with their whims and alternatives. They are normally right and in no way take responsibility for his or her mistakes. Matter of reality, they find it very hard to make an apology for the incorrect they have performed. They constantly have ready excuses accessible.

In searching out to manipulate people and conditions, they're conspiring and scheming most of the time. They create lies to govern and lie to people irrespective of who gets damage. Selfish human beings with this trait lack empathy in their relationships due to the fact they care extra approximately their self-photograph and that they have the insatiable choice of creating the vicinity revolve round them.

Characteristic # five. Selfishness breeds harm. It is inherent for egocentric people who've this trait to be unloving and uncaring. They do now not care in the event that they've damage others because of the reality all they need is all that topics and no individual else. They no longer frequently show sympathy, expertise and compassion towards others and what is taking place round them. They are detached to what is taking vicinity to important human beings and the arena spherical them. They ultimately damage humans due to their self-centeredness and their inability to love and take care of others.

Chapter 14: Understanding Selfish People

Before we are capable of keep away from deal with selfish people or forestall being selfish ourselves, we want to recognize the realities surrounding egocentric people.

Reality # 1. All selfish people aren't always lousy. Although it's miles proper that egocentric human beings constantly have a propensity to reputation on their goals and hobby, one have to understand that no longer every person who are egocentric are downright evil. They are egocentric but they do now not recommend or intend damage to others. By spotting this, we offer them room to appearance past themselves. We encourage them to create a balance among themselves and others.

Reality # 2. The human beings you recall selfish aren't robotically the trouble. We should recognise and be for the purpose that people have become selfish due to conditions and people round them. We might possibly have encouraged, pushed and driven them to be egocentric. We should ask ourselves the question, "Have I contributed to this person's selfish inclinations?" Many instances, human beings have become selfish because of the reality they were seemed absolutely egocentric despite the fact that they had been in reality searching for to shield themselves or because of the truth they have been moreover disadvantaged of the love and expertise they deserve.

Reality # three. Selfish humans want to understand and take delivery of that they may be selfish. Recognizing and accepting one's selfishness takes plenty of honesty and braveness. When we confront our inadequacies, we need time to simply accept them. Courage, the choice to change and develop are conditions for egocentric people to accept that they'll be egocentric. Selfish folks that are without a doubt inspired to alternate will need to be sincere and obvious approximately their inadequacies for alternate to occur.

Reality # 4. We can't expect selfish humans to alternate in a unmarried day. Getting rid of our selfishness isn't always a one shot deal. It isn't some factor that has a right away solution. It is a manner and the greater egocentric you are, the extra time may be had to cope with one's selfishness. Where the whole lot is instant in recent times, we want everything to be resolved proper away. Any recuperation requires time and a manner. Selfishness is something that wants to be handled, dedication, endurance and consistency.

Reality # 5. Some egocentric humans are obviously impolite and cruel. Some egocentric people are surely evil. These selfish human beings need others to fail and undergo. They discover fantastic pleasure in the difficulties, misfortunes and sufferings of others which often they've plotted. There is this monster in them that deliberately and maliciously attempting to find to malign others because of envy, jealousy and absence of self assurance. They hate the idea that others are higher, extra executed and greater favored than them.

Chapter 15: Why Stop Being Selfish

It have become important to recognize what selfishness is and what it is not in the preceding chapters. How are we able to cope with the selfishness in us or the selfishness in others until we apprehend and apprehend what we're speakme about? In the final bankruptcy, we may be managing the manner to forestall being egocentric. But before that, why save you being egocentric?

From the very beginning, we were clear approximately this. You want to stand out and also you need to be the great a number of the relaxation. You need to be a winner in any other case you need to be the pinnacle salesman. Maybe you aspire to be the brand new manager of your agency, there is no individual stopping you. You deserve it!

However, to stand out and be a winner does no longer advocate that it's fine about me, myself and I. Otherwise, you're missing out on the maximum essential subjects in life. You're lacking out at the happiness brought approximately with the useful useful resource of our worthwhile relationships with others.

When you exclude others, being a winner doesn't make experience. Your triumphs emerge as meaningless due to the fact you do not have every body to percentage your victory with. You do not have everybody to rejoice your pride. You recognise which you've made it to the top on this crazy international however you're despised and not cherished.

Why stop being selfish? The answer is apparent. Your bullying didn't art work, your situations, lies and manipulation didn't artwork as nicely. You can't be insecure, scared, hurting and on my own all your existence. You can't sulk and stay inside the darkish all the time.

It's time to redirect your internal compass. Be loose! Start using this mantra, "I am not scared, I am assured, I do no longer create partitions, I gather bridges, I am no longer searching, I breathe abundance, I am now not selfish, I provide."

Chapter 16: How To Stop Being Selfish

This is a desire you need to make nowadays. Only you've got got the electricity to loose yourself from the bondage of selfishness. You need to be excessive fine and assured that the attempt you put in these days technique the beginning of a present day you. You need to need a lifestyles sealed with right and exciting relationships due to the fact you have got taken the formidable step to prevent being egocentric. If you agree with that you have the power to unfastened your self from selfishness, it's time to redirect your inner compass. It's time to save you being egocentric.

Guide # 1 towards redirecting your inner compass. Recognize and get hold of which you are egocentric, that is vital and easy. Healing can most effective come approximately while we understand that we're sick. You can't treatment a few issue that you do no longer or refuse to understand exists. It takes an ozOf honesty and braveness to extensively identified and accept one's selfishness. To help you see through your selfishness, you have to look decrease again and bear in mind the regularly and activities you've got have been given been selfish to others. Face your inadequacies and allow bypass.

Guide #2 toward redirecting your inner compass. Let move of the me, myself and I. Stop believing that the sector revolves around you. Set the me, myself and I in you free. Allowing others to occupy a few region to your inner you does no longer advocate you want to prevent being worried for yourself, your wishes and pursuits. Letting circulate of the me, myself and I does not endorse I am reducing myself off but it's recognizing that I am not the center of the the entirety, and everyone, and accepting that I do not need to manipulate others. This have to in reality advise taking time to concentrate to others through letting others quit their sentences with none interruptions. This can also require from you to transport the extra mile of placing a person else's desires in advance than your personal desires. Parents are notable at this. They generally have their kids's goals in mind in spite of the truth that it method to sacrifice over and over again. Try from time to time to recall one-of-a-type human beings's goals earlier than your very personal. You is probably amazed which you truly did yourself a pick out.

Guide #three towards your internal compass. Get rid of your extra luggage. For you to move earlier, you want to unfastened yourself from your doubts, hurts and fears. Get rid of something that stops, drags and slows you from starting up yourself to others. The goal is to move in advance with out that extra weight, so it's far less difficult to get in your tour spot. Moving on creates happiness, have a bias for motion. Take the initiative of saying sorry to a pal or member of the family, and allow pass of the damage. You'll be surprised that you've absolutely freed yourself from sleepless nights. Give up the control for your relationship at the side of your companion. Learn to pay attention, to apprehend and to attain out extra frequently. You may be grateful which you've actually allowed your partner to concentrate, to understand and obtain out to you extra as properly.

Make a list of your doubts, hurts and fears and face them head on. Break those partitions that protected you from failing or getting harm all over again. Instead, collect bridges that allows you to will will let you create opportunities and worthwhile relationships with others and advantage unrealized plans. You may be in awe that there can be a stunning international awaiting you, which you had been deprived of due to that greater luggage.

Guide #4 towards your internal compass. Make a gratitude listing. It is less hard to be exact to others if you are aware existence has been extraordinary to you. Don't waste it slow complaining about the topics which you do now not have or wallowing on unfulfilled dreams. Stop comparing your existence to others, don't live on the "if simplest".

Instead, make it a addiction to write down down or don't forget all the proper and happy belongings you've been through in some unspecified time inside the destiny of the day before you retire for the night time. You will understand how existence and people have been so right and generous to you. Be grateful and make it a cause to be true and generous to others day after today.

Thank people usually for the good they've achieved to you. Often, it isn't sufficient to say thank you. For the companion who in no way receives tired cooking your meals every day, deliver her a hug. For the officemate who helped you end a task, supply him a espresso. For the plumber who got here to restore your sink at an inconvenient time, provide him a groovy drink. There are instances even as you moreover may additionally want to pay it forward. Do now not underestimate the brilliant energies you create whilst you recognize a way to be thankful with the every day miracles surrounding you.

Guide #five towards redirecting your internal compass. Resolve to devote your self for your course of action. Take complete duty and do now not appearance again. Commitment is a massive phrase that calls for each guts and diligence and exchange is in no way clean. There can be days at the identical time as you feel your self falling down, at the equal time as you're honestly too lazy or tired to artwork on you. Be organization collectively with your desire to trade and live focused, take the motive force's seat and look at your route. Do no longer permit discouragement or laziness set in, cultivate the electricity of interest.

Surround your self with excessive great thoughts and beneficiant humans. We are very plenty defined and caused with the buddies we preserve. Spending time spherical oldsters which can be giving and being concerned will inspire us to do the identical. Cultivate the electricity of attraction

Guide #6 in the path of redirecting your inner compass. Be notable, it is able to be critical to exchange your mindset at the identical time as giving and sharing. You will gain extra happiness via giving to others. I clearly preferred this track when I have grow to be a baby about having something and giving it away. It says that giving is like a magic penny that at the same time as you on hold tight of it, you acquired't get any. But at the identical time as you lend it, spend it and provide it away, it'll come lower back to you. Don't fear an excessive amount of however pick to be the thrilled giver. You are a winner, offer it your best shot. What you gain will especially rely on how an entire lot you are inclined to invest.

Guide #7 toward redirecting your inner compass. Apply the strength of empathy. Be privy to the people and conditions spherical you. You will see the difference while you attempt to walk a mile in each unique man's footwear or what we name to empathize. It will assist that while you discovered about patients of the current storm that left people devastated, you trust which you are the only left and now not the usage of a shelter to cowl you, no clothes to location on and no meals to eat. Imagine that no individual cared that will help you in this terrible need. How would this make you experience?

It is much less complex to attain out to others when we apprehend the situations they will be going thru. We are moved to offer a person begging for meals at the same time as we understand how it's far to be hungry. We are inspired to help a blind guy from crossing the road whilst we feel how it is to walk in darkness.

Guide #eight towards redirecting your internal compass. Increase your capability to love each day and do not set conditions while you provide. Create a list of what are you willing to perform these days and maintain on increasing them each day. Love knows no limits, you may begin from easy acts of giving until your comprehend that your coronary coronary heart has emerge as larger and large that giving truly flows through you obviously.

Here is a list of things to begin with:

1. Today, will I say thanks to a friend.

2. I will take time to pay attention to my brother.

3. I will volunteer for a network assignment.

four. I will percent my sources whenever there may be an possibility.

5. I will simplest purchase the things that I want.

6. I will be a part of a set hobby interior my community.

7. I will allow my coworker take the middle degree.

eight. I will invite my grandparents over for dinner.

Keep growing your listing. The maximum critical detail proper right here is that you create possibilities for your self to provide until it turns into a addiction.

Guide #nine in the direction of redirecting your internal compass. Be guided by way of others and be open to comments. A lot of humans need to peer you benefit your purpose, allow them to guide and help you. You cannot do it on my own, you need others to assist and cheer you on as you embark in this tough adventure of seeking to prevent being selfish. You need others to accompany and inspire you, they may be your own family, your friends, your colleagues, your buddies or all people. Do not take offense even as people attempt to suggest strategies you could better benefit your dreams, even as they may be trying to remind you which you need to get decrease lower back at the right song, or when they criticize you from deviating out of your of aim of changing the selfish you.

Guide #10 in the direction of redirecting your internal compass. Don't give up. This will not be an in a single day device, stick with it. Don't surrender even as you deliver way, get up and strive yet again. You may be a higher, happier you in the end.

Chapter 17: Terminating The Toxicity In Your Life

Remembering that I'll be lifeless quick is the most critical device I've ever encountered to help me make the massive alternatives in lifestyles. Because nearly the entirety — all outside expectations, all pleasure, all fear of embarrassment or failure – these items genuinely fall away inside the face of lack of existence, leaving first-rate what's definitely vital. Remembering that you're going to die is the great manner I apprehend to keep away from the entice of wondering you've got some thing to lose. You are already naked. There is not any cause now not to comply together with your coronary coronary heart."

– Steve Jobs

Your life is getting shorter thru the second and you can't give you the cash for to permit it's hijacked by means of the use of a toxic man or woman. Your assignment consequently is to understand and dispose of them out of your lifestyles.

A pragmatic and motivating location to start is to do a people audit and workout whom you definitely like and whoever makes your coronary coronary heart sink while you consider them. List your family, buddies and friends, divide them into must haves, incredible to knows, neutrals and toxics. Obviously wonderful techniques can be vital for every type, however this workout makes you bear in mind your relationships in a completely focussed manner.

Be brutally honest and sensible approximately this. This is your life, proper?

Make your hit listing of the Toxics and be unambiguous. If you have got any doubts, recollect the terrible impact they have got on you, and that after you are rid of them, the Toxics will quick find out others to abuse or to enroll in their pity party. They become the monkey on someone else's again, but now not yours.

If that idea inspires and excites you, growing a notable coronary heart-warming experience of treatment and completely happy delight, you recognize what you need to do. Also you will be helping the Toxic to discover greater interesting and captivating sports in vicinity of spend all their time annoying you.

A win-win state of affairs for all, do you not agree?

Consider the usage of the Friend Ranking Quadrant (FRQ) to benefit a practical appraisal of your buddies and buddies.

Friend Ranking Quadrant	
Must Have	Nice to Know
Neutral	ToXiC

You'll rapid see who provides price on your existence — excellent buddies who are generally there for you who supply joy into your life and who you usually live up for seeing. And as a corollary, people who detract fee — even thinking about them creates a darkish terrible cloud over your head.

Closely don't forget the humans to your existence and schooling session in which they match in the quadrant. This adds clarity if finished with honesty and the Toxic field on the decrease proper hand aspect bureaucracy your hit list.

If you need a golden rule if you want to healthy the whole thing, that is it: do not have something for your homes that you do not understand to be useful or consider to be lovely."

— William Morris

William Morris, the touchstone of eloquence on topics of indoors format and the artwork of residing moreover offers a marvellous philosophy to use to the humans on your lifestyles. Where do they stand in terms of together with rate, being useful, beautiful or just existence enhancingly notable to be spherical?

So you've worked out your awesome pals, humans you actually care approximately and so forth. Then there's the people you're happy to hang around with however aren't too near, and then there are those whom you tolerate or are detached to.

Now, what's left on the save you of this manner of distillation? Your Toxic hit list that's what. Consider those people and how they make you feel. If there's no ambiguity about their constant bad effect, they may be those you want to jettison.

There is a developing style closer to minimalism, decluttering and simplifying topics (america small residence movement is a charming and sustainable instance of this). People are beginning to see the benefits of cutting rate and clutter and stripping their existence to a few necessities that upload and beautify charge.

The stuff you used to very very own, now they personal you."

— Chuck Palahniuk

Remember, the extra possessions you have got have been given, the more they very personal you – you want to pay for their acquisition, renovation, renovation, area to preserve them in, insurance and so on. Then you worry in the occasion that they get stolen or broken or, within the case of an funding', lose price. If you are into Buddhism, you can view this as a salutary instance of the Second Noble Truth – that suffering is because of craving, attachment and lack of know-how. Psychologists call this 'hedonic model'. The greater you have, the extra you want, and the more you switch out to be disappointed with what you've got already got, accordingly developing a vicious circle.

The equal goes for people for your existence. Are the excessive protection and ugly ones sincerely well worth the funding in time, power and emotional determination?

No rely in which or what, there are makers, takers, and fakers."

— Robert Heinlein

This illuminating quote from one of the masters of Science Fiction additionally may be used to help grade human beings you recognize and examine their tiers of fee or toxicity. The charge that human beings add to your existence may be remarkable or horrible. Think about whom you recognise and training session which of the three they'll be. Do they take extra than they offer, are they fake to you, or do they make your life a pride to experience?

Are there any overlaps? Imagine this as a Venn diagram. Most people may have a aggregate of those tendencies, in various proportions.

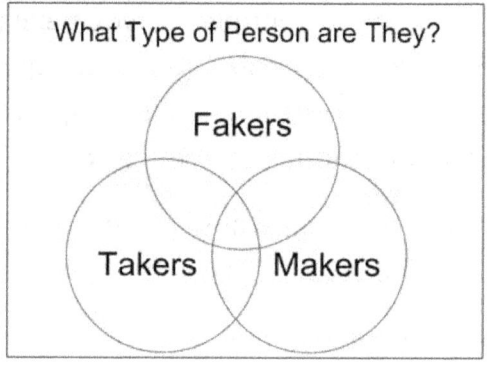

In truth, which can be you?

Chapter 18: Toxic Traits

I've positioned out that people will forgive what you stated, humans will forget about what you in all likelihood did, but people will in no manner forget the manner you made them sense."

– Maya Angelou

A toxic man or woman may be a few or a mixture of the subsequent – it's pretty probably that you may add many more descriptors, but those are a number of the signifiers to look out for. Most poisonous sorts will encompass severa of these traits.

If you surely appropriate fortune out, you'll get one who is an unholy and unprecedented combination of all of them, a self-perfected priest or priestess of the art work of toxicity, the baneful and baleful Buddha who constantly reminds you of the ignoble reality of (your) struggling (but neglects the helping you find the enlightened answer bit). This Toxic is explored in detail final of all within the Toxic Taxonomy and is referred to as the Meta-Toxic.

These tendencies can be explored in more detail as we meet every of the 9 contributors of the Toxic Taxonomy. Consider this financial disaster a place to begin of behaviours that must offer you with a warning to a potential Toxic.

Now it's time to bungee dive down the rabbit hole of the reprehensible reprobates. Here are some of the principle inclinations – enjoy unfastened to feature your very personal.

Abusive and bullying – this includes passive aggressive behaviour similarly to the more obvious and overt kinds. The Toxic can also inn to all way of threats to get their personal manner, relying on their reading of you. This is probably the way they behave towards you all the time, or part of a cocktail of behaviours that they may be trying out to look what works super of their dealings with you. This manner, they may form a sample and exercising consultation which of your warmth buttons they may be capable of hit to try to benefit an final results that they preference.

Boring and banal – all they eye-glazingly and will-to-stay sappingly talk about is "me, me, me". This is one of the primary traits of a Necrotic Narcissist, but some of the opposite Toxics aren't proof towards hogging centre degree and playing to the gallery.

Cowardly – can and could act within the again of your over again but deflate without hassle if challenged, that is once they descend into self-pity and angst, which of route, is your fault. Some Toxics will feign cowardice, the usage of it as a weapon to region you off your shield to be able to retrench and strike lower decrease returned at a later date.

Depressing – Toxics pride in dragging you all the way down to their degree and attempt to maintain you there. Continued exposure exacerbates this tendency and may mire you in a disempowered us of a. This may additionally need to make it difficult to do so, and disempowering you is but a few different manner that the Toxic tries to play you, because it makes you more malleable and masses a great deal much less likely to interrupt out from their presence and feature an impact on.

Destructive – this may be of your fitness, happiness and sanity. The Toxic is a pernicious have an effect on, and the longer they remain to your life, the greater poor their effect upon you. They can turn out to be a longstanding hassle that debilitates you, like a chronic illness. But there are strategies to deal with them – they don't ought to sap your physical, emotional and psychological strength.

Dishonest – the Toxic will do whatever to get their personal manner. For them, the reality is definitely relative and is to be bent and repurposed so as for them collect their dreams of their relationship with you. Treat something they're pronouncing or do with immoderate caution, specially at the same time as they will be talking about "what other humans said".

Emotional and Energy Vampires – Toxics can drain your of energy and desire. You can nearly experience your will to stay being sapped with the aid in their regular neediness or hectoring. They feed upon your emotional electricity and behavior, and you could almost see them excessive-fiving as their effect grows and that they score vital mental hits.

Guilt inducing – to a Toxic, everything is your fault, and a few difficulty has passed off that reputedly blights their life isn't always some thing to do with them. The idea of private obligation appears alien to them, and some of them pretty actually assume that the world in elegant and also you specially owe them a residing. Imagine a self-obsessed parasite that drains you of power at the same time as blaming you for his or her lifestyles scenario; and you could see how poor their impact can be.

Hoovers – the kind of Toxic who you located has lengthy passed out of your life who will then try and touch you on a 'large' date, birthday, anniversary, Christmas, New Year, in an attempt to make touch at a time that have come to be, in their perception of the area, "specific to every folks". This Toxic is unprepared to permit pass or skip on, despite the fact that that could be the maximum practical and collectively beneficial element for all sports to do. They see advantageous dates as 'critical' and may be marking the time until the ones take location, as they resonate in the Toxic's psyche and they wish that a similar resonance is taking location with you.

Ignoble and unprincipled – irrespective of how ridiculous they seem to every body else, this does not prevent them drawing close at you. Some Toxics have a distorted and as an alternative embarrassing experience of self. Their immaturity is obvious when they revert to childish behaviour within the event that they don't get what they need. Expect a chain of socially maladapted tantrums when you have the misfortune to have this shape of poisonous man or woman for your existence.

Invites you to a the front row seat at their pity party – attempts to keep you in a disempowered kingdom. Certain Toxics seem to get off on sharing their very very own distress with one of a kind people and you can get a cluster of them sharing their personal tragedies and misfortunes. They will try and outdo each distinctive in a bid for sympathy and feed off such public presentations of emotional incontinence. Positive questioning is kept away from here, and all and sundry of an fine mind-set is encouraged to keep away from such delinquent activities, as it's clean that terrible questioning may be contagious.

Irresponsible – Toxics no longer often acquire their duty for his or her very own life and u . S . A . Of mind, as it's your complete fault, proper? It's tough to purpose with this sort of desirable judgment, and it's very clean to lose staying strength with such thinking, so your most effective desire is to avoid such people.

Judgemental – Toxics regularly display off a inflexible and inflexible view of the location, looking you to paste to their particularist view of the sector, even within the face of all proof to the alternative. It's their manner or the motorway; so if you are confronted thru this kind of, slam the pedal to the metal and go away at excessive pace.

Manipulative – they will use any way to benefit and supply a lift in your compliance. This is a feature of all Toxics – they'll set up exclusive techniques and some can be a whole lot more effective than others of their subtlety and capacity effectiveness.

Martyrs — slaves to the blame endeavor, however some exceptional manner to make you accountable and compliant. Toxics will try to engage your sympathy and give you a potential backstory as to why you should experience sympathy and have interaction with them. Creating a revel in of guilt, indebtedness and obligation for your thing is truly taken into consideration one in all their strategies.

Narcissists — extra approximately "me, me, and me" pondered through the mirror of their very very own neediness and egotism. The Necrotic Narcissist is the critical trouble exemplar of this poisonous fashion; but it exists to severa degrees in they all. Genuine coronary heart-felt empathy isn't their robust in shape, despite the fact that a Meta-Toxic may be very powerful at feigning it.

Needy — latch onto you as they lack internal clear up. This neediness can be very sporting, or maybe if you are to start with sympathetic and have compassion, it brief turns into obvious that that is a Toxic Trope that they constantly play.

Self-unfavourable – they'll moreover take you down with them, so in case your intuition for self-preservation is strong, avoidance is your best practical technique. Some Toxics have fragmented personalities and appear like oblivious to the harm that they're doing to themselves and others. Others appear to get off on such subjects. Self-harming or attempted suicide aren't unknown with some Toxics, who will take themselves to the issue of self-annihilation which will attempt to paintings your nobler dispositions of compassion and kindness.

Solipsistic – the whole lot is prepared them, and don't you apprehend it. This shape of Toxic is extraordinarily wearing and thinks and acts as though they may be the very centre of the universe. Getting close to them is like drawing close to the occasion horizon surrounding a black hollow – get too near and you can get sucked in to a parallel universe of Toxicity.

Takes offence – at the slightest problem. Some Toxics are very effortlessly indignant and you are without a doubt strolling on eggshells spherical them. Volatile Volcanoes are an excellent example, although you'll additionally discover that most Toxics can without issue discover a few element to take offence at, and could react in numerous, generally unpleasant methods if this seems to reveal as much as them. Their perceptions of being angry appear to live in a country of excessive cortisol pushed alertness, that's distinctly sporting to those round them.

Undermining – commonly looking to get you down. This toxic trait is invidious and wearing, and there can appear like no comfort from it. Clearly dwelling with such someone is most likely to have a completely terrible psychological effect on the associate, who can also should very severely weigh up the professionals and cons of persisting in this sort of courting. Let's face it; 24x7x365 (that's 31,536,000 seconds a three hundred and sixty five days, parents, besides you're fortunate enough to be experiencing a Leap Year) of undermining is not conducive to nicely fitness.

Undesirable – tries to appear your friend but is some thing however, and most people with any self-attention avoid them just like the proverbial plague. Insincerity and a loss of authenticity characterise Toxics who display off this trait. They'll don't have any inhibitions about lying, backstabbing or spreading faux facts about you.

Upset constantly – because of you or any character else, some unique way to try to manage you through the pity birthday party trope. This is virtually a form of mental manipulation and can be extremely embarrassing if it takes area in public. Some Toxics don't have any social self-popularity and couldn't hesitate to play their face in front of different human beings, trying to get them onside and on message which will manage you.

Victims – of something that lets in them get their way. Some Toxics are expert sufferers and function perfected that function. They play the sympathy trope for all it's properly well worth and have a cautiously rehearsed backstory that they're best too inclined to percentage. These human beings can be very whiney, their neediness constantly grates and is regularly contemplated of their body language and the way they express themselves.

Chapter 19: Toxic Taxonomy (The Noxious Nine)

Begin each day by means of the use of telling yourself: these days I may be assembly with interference, ingratitude, insolence, disloyalty, ill-will, and selfishness – they all because of the offenders' lack of statistics of what is ideal or evil."

— Marcus Aurelius

You may be an amazingly remarkable character, wholesome, wholesome and buoyant with a top notch outlook on life. Your past is terrific and you've got were given fond reminiscences of all of the first-rate critiques you've cherished. Your future is so vivid that you've have been given to don clothier shades.

There's genuinely one detail which you need to kind out inside the gift. There's someone, some aspect that's taking up an excessive amount of of your irreplaceable time and strength. This has manifested as an emotional blight, a mental contagion that desires to be eliminated from your existence. You apprehend you need to have handled this situation in advance. You're completely conscious which you've permit it hang around too lengthy and all at once, after a protracted length of recognition, you've reached the tipping component. It's time to perform that, to regain manage, to remove that pernicious have an impact on.

You apprehend that positive human beings all of the time make you feel terrible. You might be an idealist however some humans should make you experience delusional or lacking in smarts. Maybe you satisfaction yourself to your independence, adulthood and self-reliance; but while uncovered to a specific form of character you experience like you're reverting to a early life united states of disempowerment.

You recognize all this, rationally and intuitively, but you still allow certain human beings, usually known as Toxics, to do it. Which way they have got greater strength over you than you do over your self.

Currently, at the least, it's your name, right?

If you comprehend this in yourself and recognize you're being negatively impacted through Toxics, it's time to redress the stability.

These people may be described as Toxic or poisonous personalities as they disturb your equilibrium, equanimity, and impact upon your happiness and probable your sanity. They may have an effect for your existence and vanity and it's been argued that continued exposure to them and the stress they'll be capable of reason may shorten your lifestyles.

Some Toxics are very smooth to pick out early on. They exhibit a exquisite form of electricity, a body language that indicates their furtive and disloyal nature. The way they speak verbally, the terms they use and the sly look on their insincere faces reinforces the feeling that they are brilliant avoided. To any rational observer, they seem like searching out someone to control and make problem for. Most humans have a wholesome experience of self-safety and splendid self-esteem and could revel in this shape of Toxic and, like severa healthful organism that recoils from sickness, keep away from them.

Other Toxics are an entire lot savvier and greater skilful and practiced at disguising their proper nature and goals. They insinuate themselves into the lives of others and their friends, which could make it difficult to remove them without a few fallout in your social or professional lifestyles. They display who and what they're step by step, having received precious belief into who you're and the way your personality and feelings may be exploited to their very very own ends.

So the secret is to be forewarned and forearmed. You can in no manner tell at the same time as one of the more advanced Toxics might be approximately to press the flesh with you and profess to make you their notable pal. The following Toxic Taxonomy offers an intensive manual to fundamental kinds of Toxic, displaying what you want to be looking for for and while alarm bells want to begin to ring out loud and easy.

Chapter 20: The Toxic Wheel Of Misfortune

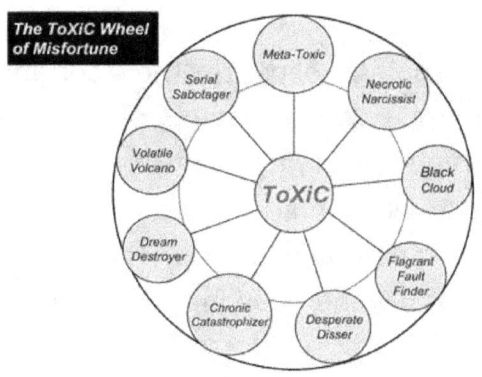

The following is a quick and impactive advent to people who may be delivered real fast now. This is the roulette wheel of the reprehensible – the Noxious Nine Toxic Types.

1. Necrotic Narcissists, Total Takers And Perennial Parasites

This vexatious model of the Toxic Taxonomy feels very self-vital and assumes that they may be the centre of the world – theirs, yours and every one else's. And of path, they'll be able to't wait to proportion this profound however exquisite belief with you or anyone else unfortunate sufficient to be interior earshot. They assume you to comply with this view.

Energy sapping solipsists, they continuously strive to pull you into their orbit. 'Me, me, me' is their unvarying mantra, 'yawn, yawn, yawn' is most human beings's inevitable and often on the spot response. There are some similarities to the drawing near Meta-Toxic, besides that those Necrotic Narcissists will not often attempt to manage you with flattery. Nor will they ever faux that it's to your hobbies to do what they want. Meta-Toxics are flawlessly capable of doing each seamlessly and resultseasily and are in most respects a savvier, extra alternatively evolved form of Toxic. The type of aspect a Necrotic Narcissist would like to be, within the event that they have been self-aware, advocated, sufficiently smart, and had greater social abilties.

The Necrotic Narcissist is consequently a more obvious and lots plenty a good deal much less subtle Toxic than the Meta-Toxic.

Necrotic Narcissists will be inclined to be without troubles diagnosed early on the connection. Their long-winded monologues are peppered with the phrases 'I' and 'me' and they may be addicted to the non-public pronoun in all its office paintings – interactive speak is some issue they have got no longer begun to apprehend, no matter the reality that they may be privy to its existence. If they have been to get hold of a non-public venture announcement it would be 'I count on, I yap, I bore on', even though in reality a Necrotic Narcissist has such little self-interest that the query may want to in no manner coalesce in their minds.

And of direction, having little feel of humour, there'd be no doubt of the sort of gentle, self-deprecating self diss that maximum individuals who don't take ourselves too notably are pretty happy to provide you with to function a few lubrication to social engagement. Their body language indicates a lack of in a polite way mirroring the nuances of different humans's behaviour. Their brains don't seem to have produced reflect neurons in any big amount.

The Necrotic Narcissist indicates disinterest in the contributions of whomsoever they'll be addressing, and may't wait to move off on a tangent of their private. You would probably as well located them on a soapbox and go away them to get on with it, no matter the reality that they'd quickly get disillusioned at the dearth of an target market. Active listening isn't always their strong factor, as they will be simply watching for any opportunity to butt in and interrupt the glide of a verbal exchange to supply numerous of their self-focused and forever uninspiring and unoriginal insights into the place.

If they ever take a breather and ask a few aspect approximately you, it's due to the fact they want a few records or maybe every different opinion on which to preserve even more 'me me moi mwah mwah' stuff. You need to almost consider the slogan 'it's all about me, me, me' in a massive pinnacle case emboldened font emblazoned on a T-blouse they proudly game. Enter a communication with them and it's like turning a key that that gadgets a hint clockwork canine off yapping. The more they expound upon themselves, the more specific humans flip off and music out, or enter a catatonic trance.

If they have got a blog or on line journal, it's far going to be all about them, notwithstanding the truth that they high-quality have an goal marketplace of 1 because of the reality the incessant me-ism alienates anyone who has the misfortune to come upon it. All of which could depart them chuntering and fuming by myself, all the time on the out of doors. Of direction of their minds it's generally the fault of various human beings that this happens, and has now not some thing to do with their moves or behaviour.

The Necrotic Narcissist needs that everybody else is interested in his or her life, regardless of how prosaic or banal. To say they've got excessive expectancies of the way humans need to react to them or wallow in entitlement problems is like making the observation that dogs have a propensity to bark. If their puppy stick insect dies they expect an navy of grief counsellors to attain to console them within the ensuing months of suffering their loss.

Their personal grief eclipses troubles along with weather exchange or human rights violations. They anticipate anyone else to boogie on down and be a part of their pity birthday celebration at boohoohoosville, preferably bringing some bottles. Not most effective do they assume compassion, however they need it smeared throughout their supposedly broken and bawling psyche, a good deal as you can beautify your morning toast with butter and honey.

Don't inform humans your issues. Half of them received't care and the rest will chortle." The Necrotic Narcissist doesn't appear to have heard of this quip. Or perhaps they have got, however experience that their troubles function in this kind of cosmic scale of importance that everybody will step lower back in awe, amazement, sympathy and compassion. Or they could take the view that any interest is higher than none, and that it's better to be vilified, pitied or derided than disregarded. Dignity and the calm acceptance of the arena as it's far, in preference to the way you need it to be, are not characteristics of this sort of Toxic.

Let's say that you have had enough of 1 and decide to inform them how they make you experience – that every one the self-focused stuff at your fee is certainly wearing you and everyone else inside the region down. You decide to have a rational heart to coronary heart with them and provide an motive in the back of how they make you experience. Off you skip on your great pop-psychology and empathetic negotiation mode, trying now not to disappointed them or be perceived as attacking their fragile ego. They stand there as you utter your cautiously organized script, and they appear to take some of this on board – perhaps the bizarre nod, in all likelihood an 'a-ha' or , and the body language seems congruent. You suppose you're making a few headway and stop for a second or to take stock and possibly even permit your self a small smile of triumph and remedy.

But wait! Faster than a fighter jet growing a sonic boom as it bursts thru the sound barrier, you've given them a few component on which to hang an encyclopaedic and epic monologue of self-justification and self-pity. If you have got tears, prepare to have them forcibly extracted now. "What approximately me?" they opine, salty fluids tragically forming in their eyes, their lips quivering with emotion. "What about the manner I enjoy. Nobody ever takes MY emotions beneath attention. Do you recognise, really the opportunity day I have become considering this and I got here to the choice that..." You can possibly write the relaxation of the script right proper right here, it sincerely is why coping with them is fraught with problems. Avoid Necrotic Narcissists in any respect costs as their very presence brings you down. They have a perpetual entitlement hassle and no longer anything is ever sufficient for them. They will take the whole thing they're capable of. And then assume greater – undergo in thoughts them as an super and lousy emo vampire.

They'll typically aspect out your indiscretions and those of others at the identical time as every blithely ignoring or hyping up their non-public faults and then looking ahead to compassion or expertise. They're so interesting and unique they suppose they deserve your finer traits being spent on them, proper? Attention is what they are looking for, and depriving them of it like doing away with the toys from an over emotional, spoilt and not terribly clever infant – you can guarantee a protracted winded and slow burning tantrum developing real fast now.

The more those Toxic types get away with behaving as they do, the extra they may be advocated to hold. They're oblivious to their behaviour and its results on others and consequently deny, severely downplay or violently reject this being talked about to them. They get frequently more irritated and competitive whilst neglected, humming away like a fly trapped internal an the alternative way up glass. The truth hurts, in fact.

They additionally get worse as they grow to be old – me-ism is not a excellent that matures like a pleasing wine – and they usually have a tendency to have a greater, cumulative effect as time progresses. It's like having a car alarm screeching away outdoor your bed room window that in no way stops. As your lifestyles receives shorter, you want to make bigger techniques for managing this

Toxic type and urgent the buttons that eject them out of your lifestyles.

Why are they known as Necrotic Narcissists? In the Greek fable, Narcissus fell in love together together with his good-looking reflected photo in a pool of water and turned into so absorbed via himself that he not noted to eat or drink, wasted away and died. This Toxic is in a love affair with themself at the price of all others, which has a tendency to reason them to as an opportunity dull, boring and uninspiring industrial organisation agency.

It's uncommon that they have any near buddies – there's now not a few factor internal them for every person else to shape a bond with – and any wonderful one-of-a-type has lengthy in the past placed to music them out once they start out genuinely certainly one of their invariable screeds. An unfortunate listener can be feeling that they are death of boredom and dropping away, possibly eaten from indoors by the usage of flesh ingesting bacteria of the psyche, sooner or later the necrotic nomenclature.

There is a very smooth difference among this Toxic and a person with charisma. A charismatic character owns the undivided attention of these whom they address, whether or not or not or no longer an character or a big auditorium, due to the reality they include the goal market, either via appealing with them, selectively the use of eye contact or with the useful resource of sheer strain of presence. They seem to take a real and genuine hobby.

The charismatic character makes use of the sniper's rifle technique, just so each person feels that they are being addressed at once. The Toxic rather makes use of the blunderbuss or cudgel, by no means appealing with all of us else and honestly blasting a payload of silly talk in any route so that you can are searching for attention and spot what sticks. Subtle they may be no longer. A deluded Necrotic Narcissist may also see him- or herself as having air of thriller, irrespective of all proof to the other. The reviews of others are very no longer regularly taken on board, till to disagree with them and release into similarly sick-knowledgeable rhetoric.

Necrotic Narcissists also are Total Takers and Perennial Parasites. As an extended way as those humans are involved some thing you do is by no means enough, the entirety is your fault and they in no way take shipping of obligation for something – ever. The Necrotic Narcissist is the remaining blame gamer. They greedily draw close the whole thing you provide in phrases of physical and emotional output. They call for increasingly more from you whilst providing you with not whatever in go back besides for a sense of being clearly used.

Once they've worn-out you clearly, this Toxic Incubus movements unexpectedly directly to the subsequent host, at the same time as blaming you for now not being a sympathetic or statistics listener.

Dealing With Necrotic Narcissists, Total Takers And Perennial Parasites

There are a few strategies you can strive in advance than ditching the ones humans as quickly as and for all (need to that be viable). One technique is the usage of the phrase NO – preserve saying it until they get the message which you're not prepared to offer into unreasonable needs. You can also provide those people a business enterprise, forceful verbal (non-violent obviously) slap down in the event that they bypass your limitations. Which, given what they may be like, they'll. The idea of obstacles is as alien to them as deep sea diving is to a cat.

You can also control your response to them and that consists of your expectancies of them. Let's face it, those humans are far too emotionally immature to provide some thing to you – they clearly take. So in case you need to cling with them be given which you aren't going to get out of the connection what you put in.

Don't anticipate extra from the ones people than they are able to giving. Get your wishes met a few one of a kind location. Don't base your vanity or self confidence on them setting you first every so often or perhaps recognising which you have goals of your very

very very own. That can simplest bring about unhappiness. Accept that for them you only exist to (self) serve.

There is one extra trick that you strive earlier than ejecting them out of your existence and this is displaying them how treating you better is in their exquisite hobbies. That's if you could get them to pay sufficient hobby to you to pay interest you out earlier than interrupting and talking approximately themselves. They might possibly even increase empathy and display a few hobby in someone apart from himself or herself.

www.ingramcontent.com/pod-product-compliance
Lightning Source LLC
Chambersburg PA
CBHW050359120526
44590CB00015B/1756